Oceanic Oases

Under Threat

Climate Change and its Toll on Mediterranean,
Gulf, and Indian Ocean Enclaves

GEW Reports & Analyses Team

Global East West

CONTENTS

Introduction

C limate change is one of the most pressing issues of our time, threatening the very fabric of our planet and the livelihoods of millions of people around the world. As a famous writer, I feel a sense of duty to address this critical issue through my writing, bringing attention to the devastating consequences of climate change and inspiring action for a more sustainable future.

The purpose of this book is to delve deep into the specific challenges that small islands and peninsulas face in the face of climate change and to explore the regional impacts within the Mediterranean, the Gulf, and the Indian Ocean. These regions are particularly vulnerable due to their geographical characteristics and their dependence on natural resources for economic and social development.

In small islands, rising sea levels present an alarming threat. These islands have limited land that is already densely populated, with many communities clustered along the coastlines. As the sea levels rise, these communities are at risk of losing their homes and even their entire islands to inundation. Furthermore, the increased vulnerability of coastal infrastructure, such as roads, bridges, and airports, threatens the mobility and connectivity of these island nations.

Peninsulas, on the other hand, face unique challenges due to their elongated landforms that are surrounded by water on three sides. The rising sea levels have a cascading impact on these regions, leading to saltwater intrusion into freshwater sources and affecting agricultural productivity and freshwater availability. Additionally, the combination of sea-level rise and extreme weather events, such as storms and hurricanes, poses a dual threat to the coastal communities of peninsulas, causing physical damage and economic losses.

The Mediterranean region occupies a prominent position within the global climate change discourse. As one of the world's biodiversity hotspots, this region faces significant challenges due to increasing temperatures and changes in precipitation patterns. The Mediterranean Sea itself acts as a climate amplifier, impacting the surrounding land masses and exacerbating the effects of climate change. The rise in temperature, coupled with decreased rainfall and an increased frequency of heatwaves and droughts, has direct consequences on agricultural productivity, water availability, and the delicate balance of regional ecosystems.

The Gulf region, comprising countries such as Saudi Arabia, Qatar, and the United Arab Emirates, faces unique climate challenges due to its desert climate and heavy reliance on fossil fuels. The extreme heatwaves experienced in this region are projected to increase in intensity and frequency as global warming continues. Heatwaves have dire consequences on human health, as well as infrastructure, including power grids and transportation systems, leading to societal disruptions and economic losses. Additionally, the Gulf region is particularly vulnerable to sea-level rise and storm surge, which pose significant risks to coastal cities and critical infrastructure.

The Indian Ocean region, consisting of islands such as the Maldives and the Seychelles, faces a multitude of climate change impacts. Rising sea levels pose an existential threat to these low-lying islands, as entire communities may be forced to abandon their homes. These island nations also face an increased frequency and intensity of tropical cyclones, leading to devastating damage and loss of life. Furthermore, coral bleaching, caused by increasing ocean temperatures, threatens the diverse marine ecosystems that these island nations depend on for tourism and fisheries.

To understand the gravity of the situation, it is crucial to examine the historical climate data and projections specific to these regions. The Mediterranean has seen an increase in temperature of around 1.5°C over the past century, affecting its delicate balance of biodiversity and regional ecosystems. The Gulf region sets records for high temperatures, with some areas experiencing temperatures above 50°C. The Indian Ocean region has witnessed a rise in ocean temperatures leading to coral bleaching events.

In response to the challenges posed by climate change, regional cooperation among Arab countries has emerged as an essential strategy for mitigation and adaptation. The Arab League, for example, has established the Arab Strategy on Climate Change, which aims to enhance communication, knowledge sharing, and capacity building among its member states. The Gulf Cooperation Council (GCC) has also taken steps to address climate change through the development of national policies, renewable energy initiatives, and water conservation measures.

However, it is important to critically analyse these policy responses, taking into consideration power structures and environmental justice within these frameworks. Often, marginalised communities bear the brunt of climate change impacts due to their limited access to resources and influence in decision-making processes. Recognising and addressing these issues is crucial in ensuring an equitable and just transition to a more sustainable future.

Furthermore, climate change is deeply interconnected with other global challenges such as conflict and migration. The scarcity of resources, including water and agricultural land, can exacerbate existing tensions and trigger conflicts, as witnessed in the Syrian civil war, where drought and agricultural collapse acted as contributing factors. Additionally, climate-induced migration is becoming a reality as people are forced to leave their homes due to rising sea levels, extreme weather events, and loss of livelihoods. Understanding the linkages between climate change, conflict, and migration is vital in developing holistic strategies that address the root causes and provide support to affected communities.

Through a selection of case studies, this book will examine the varying impacts and responses in the Mediterranean, the Gulf, and the Indian Ocean, drawing cross-regional comparisons to identify best practises and lessons learnt. It will showcase the innovative approaches taken by governments, civil society organisations, and local communities to mitigate and adapt to climate change. These case studies will provide insights into community resilience, social capital, and the importance of grassroots initiatives in addressing climate change effectively.

In conclusion, this book aims to provide a comprehensive analysis of the socio-economic impacts of climate change in Arab regions, shedding light on historical climate data, regional projections, and policy responses. It seeks to foster a sense of urgency and inspire action for a more sustainable future. By understanding the complexities and challenges faced by these vulnerable regions, we can work towards implementing effective policies, promoting regional and international cooperation, and fostering a sense of global responsibility in addressing climate change.

Let this book serve as a catalyst for change, igniting a global movement towards a more sustainable and resilient world. Together, we can make a difference in combating climate change and preserving the beauty, diversity, and stability of our planet for generations to come.

Background on Climate Change

C limate change, a complex global phenomenon, refers to long-term shifts and alterations in weather patterns and average temperatures across the globe. These changes are primarily caused by human activities, particularly the burning of fossil fuels and deforestation, which result in the release of greenhouse gases (GHGs) into the atmosphere.

The accumulation of GHGs in the Earth's atmosphere traps heat from the sun, leading to a gradual increase in global temperatures. This phenomenon, commonly known as global warming, has far-reaching consequences for the planet and its inhabitants.

Scientific research, conducted by thousands of dedicated scientists and researchers, and supported by extensive data, consistently shows that the Earth is warming at an unprecedented rate. The Intergovernmental Panel on Climate Change (IPCC), comprised of leading scientists from around the world, has provided comprehensive evidence on the causes and impacts of climate change. The IPCC's reports, which undergo rigorous peer review, serve as a vital resource for policymakers and decision-makers.

The primary cause of recent global warming is the significant increase in the concentration of GHGs since the Industrial Revolution. Carbon dioxide (CO_2), mainly emitted through the burning of fossil fuels such as coal, oil, and natural gas, is the most prominent greenhouse gas contributing to human-induced climate change. Other greenhouse gases, such as methane (CH_4) from agricultural activities, land use changes, and waste management, also play a significant role.

The consequences of climate change are wide-ranging and impact various aspects of the Earth's systems. Rising temperatures have resulted in the melting of polar ice caps and glaciers, leading to accelerated sea-level rise. This poses a significant threat to coastal regions, as higher sea levels increase the risk of flooding, inundation of low-lying areas, and coastal erosion.

Extreme weather events, including hurricanes, droughts, heatwaves, and heavy rainfall, have become more frequent and intense as a result of global warming. These events have devastating effects on communities, infrastructure, and ecosystems, leading to loss of life, displacement, and economic hardship. Additionally, changes in precipitation patterns impact water availability, agriculture, and food security, further exacerbating existing vulnerabilities.

Furthermore, climate change also affects ecosystems and biodiversity. Many species struggle to adapt to rapidly changing conditions, leading to disruptions in food chains and the loss of habitat. Coral reefs, for example, are highly sensitive to even slight increases in ocean temperatures, causing mass bleaching events that can lead to their death. Changes in ecosystems and the disruption of biodiversity have broader consequences, including impacts on human livelihoods, cultural heritage, and ecosystem services.

Recognising the urgent need to address climate change, nations around the world have come together to develop international agreements and frameworks to promote collective action. An important milestone is the Paris Agreement, adopted under the United Nations Framework Convention on Climate Change (UNFCCC) in 2015. This agreement aims to limit global temperature rise well below 2 degrees Celsius above pre-industrial levels and to pursue efforts to limit the temperature increase to 1.5 degrees Celsius. Countries are expected to regularly submit nationally determined contributions (NDCs) outlining their efforts to reduce greenhouse gas emissions and adapt to the impacts of climate change.

Understanding the background and science of climate change is essential for policymakers, scientists, and the general public in developing effective strategies to mitigate its impacts. It requires interdisciplinary collaboration and a holistic understanding of the interconnectedness of various factors contributing to climate change. Continuous research, monitoring, and modelling are vital to improving our understanding of climate dynamics, projecting future scenarios, and informing policy decisions.

In recent decades, advancements in climate science have allowed researchers to attribute specific extreme weather events to human-induced climate change, known as event attribution. This emerging field enables scientists to determine the extent to which climate change has influenced the intensity or likelihood of events like heatwaves, hurricanes, and heavy rainfall. Event attribution provides valuable insight into the increasing risks faced by communities around the world.

Climate models further enhance our understanding of climate change by simulating Earth's climate system. These models incorporate factors such as greenhouse gas emissions, atmospheric circulation, ocean currents, and solar radiation to project future climate scenarios. While models have inherent uncertainties, they contribute essential information for policy-makers and decision-makers when formulating strategies to mitigate and adapt to climate change.

The social and economic impacts of climate change are vast, affecting different regions and sectors in unique ways. Small islands and penin-sulas, particularly those in the Mediterranean, the Gulf, and the Indian Ocean regions, face specific and heightened vulnerabilities due to their geographical characteristics. These regions are prone to rising sea levels, increased heatwaves, water scarcity, and changing precipitation patterns. The impacts on these areas include threats to coastal infrastructure, loss of agricultural productivity, damage to natural ecosystems, and potential mass migration. Addressing the specific challenges faced by these regions is crucial for ensuring their sustainable development and resilience in the face of climate change.

In the following chapters, we will delve deeper into the specific chal-lenges and vulnerabilities faced by small islands and peninsulas, with a regional focus on the Mediterranean, the Gulf, and the Indian Ocean. We will examine the socio-economic impacts, historical climate data, pol-icy responses, and the theoretical framework necessary to address climate change and promote environmental justice. Through comprehensive case studies, data analysis, and exploration of best practises, we aim to provide valuable insights into the impacts and responses to climate change, as well as recommendations for future action.

THE VULNERABILITY OF SMALL ISLANDS AND PENINSULAS

S mall islands and peninsulas are particularly vulnerable to the impacts of climate change due to their unique geographic characteristics. These regions often have limited land area and are surrounded by water, making them more susceptible to rising sea levels and extreme weather events. Their vulnerability stems from a combination of factors, including their isolated nature, limited resources, and reliance on specific economic sectors.

One of the most significant threats faced by small islands and peninsulas is the rising sea levels. As global temperatures increase, glaciers and ice caps melt, causing sea levels to rise. This poses a direct threat to low-lying areas, as even small increases in sea level can lead to flooding and erosion. Small islands and peninsulas are especially at risk, as they have limited land area to retreat to or build flood protection infrastructure. The loss of coastal habitats due to rising sea levels also impacts biodiversity and ecological balance, further exacerbating the vulnerability of these regions.

Extreme weather events, such as hurricanes, typhoons, and cyclones, also pose a significant risk to small islands and peninsulas. Due to their isolated nature, these regions are often exposed to the full force of these storms. The combination of high winds and storm surges can lead to widespread devastation, causing damage to infrastructure, loss of livelihoods, and even loss of life. The recovery and reconstruction processes following these events are often challenging, given the limited resources and accessibility issues faced by these communities.

In addition to the physical impacts, small islands and peninsulas also face social and economic challenges due to climate change. Many of these regions heavily rely on tourism and agriculture, which are sensitive to climate variations. Rising temperatures, changes in rainfall patterns, and increased frequency of droughts can have a detrimental impact on local economies, affecting the livelihoods of communities. This economic vulnerability can further deepen social inequalities and exacerbate existing challenges, such as poverty and food security.

Furthermore, small islands and peninsulas often have limited resources and infrastructure to cope with the impacts of climate change. Their isolation and small populations make it difficult to access funding and resources for adaptation and mitigation measures. These regions are also more dependant on imported goods and services, making them susceptible to disruptions in supply chains caused by extreme weather events or rising sea levels. The lack of financial and technical capacity impedes their ability to implement long-term strategies to address climate change challenges effectively.

To address the vulnerability of small islands and peninsulas, it is crucial to implement comprehensive climate change adaptation and mitigation strategies. This includes developing and strengthening coastal protection measures, enhancing early warning systems, and promoting sustainable land use practises. Coastal engineering solutions, such as artificial reefs, breakwaters, and dune restoration, can provide protection against erosion and storm surge impacts. Early warning systems, coupled with robust evacuation plans, can help communities prepare for and respond to extreme events effectively. Furthermore, promoting sustainable agriculture and tourism practises that enhance resilience and reduce environmental impacts can contribute to long-term sustainability.

It is also important to provide support to small islands and peninsulas through international cooperation, financial assistance, and capacity-building initiatives. Developed nations, international organisations, and regional alliances should facilitate the transfer of financial and technical resources to these regions to enable effective climate change adaptation and mitigation efforts. This support can encompass technology transfer, funding for infrastructure development, and capacity-building programmes to enhance local knowledge and expertise in climate change-related sectors.

Additionally, it is crucial to strengthen local governance structures and establish participatory decision-making processes that involve all stakeholders in adaptation and mitigation efforts. Engaging local communities, indigenous groups, and marginalised populations in climate change planning and decision-making helps ensure that their unique knowledge, experiences, and needs are taken into account. It can also empower these communities with the necessary tools, information, and resources to adapt and build resilience to climate change impacts.

Furthermore, education and awareness campaigns play a pivotal role in enhancing resilience and understanding the implications of climate change in small islands and peninsulas. These initiatives can foster a sense of ownership and responsibility among community members, encouraging sustainable practises and fostering a culture of resilience. By promoting local knowledge, traditional practises, and innovative solutions, communities can creatively adapt to the challenges posed by climate change.

In conclusion, small islands and peninsulas are highly vulnerable to the impacts of climate change due to their unique geographic characteristics, limited resources, and dependence on specific economic sectors. Immediate action is needed to mitigate the risks and support these regions in adapting to the changing climate. By addressing their vulnerabilities through a combination of comprehensive strategies, international cooperation, financial assistance, and inclusive governance, we can ensure the resilience and sustainability of these valuable ecosystems and communities.

The Mediterranean, the Gulf, and the Indian Ocean: A Regional Focus

T o study the impacts of climate change on small islands and peninsulas, it is important to focus on specific regions that are particularly vulnerable. In this chapter, we will examine the Mediterranean, the Gulf, and the Indian Ocean, and analyse the unique challenges these regions face in relation to climate change.

The Mediterranean is known for its diverse ecosystems, rich cultural heritage, and economic vitality. However, it is also facing numerous climate-related challenges. Rising sea levels pose a threat to coastal cities and towns, leading to erosion and the potential displacement of communities. The Mediterranean region has already witnessed a rise in sea levels of 3 to 10 cm over the last century, and projections indicate further increases in the future. These rising sea levels not only directly affect coastal areas but also exacerbate the impacts of storm surges, leading to increased coastal flooding and erosion. Increasing temperatures and changing precipitation patterns can have detrimental effects on agriculture, water resources, and tourism, which are important sectors of the Mediterranean economy.

Heatwaves and droughts pose risks to agriculture, reducing crop yields and increasing the prevalence of wildfires. Southern Europe, including countries like Spain, Italy, and Greece, is experiencing more frequent and intense heatwaves, with record-breaking temperatures becoming the new norm. These heatwaves invite the spread of forest fires, putting landscapes, biodiversity, and human settlements at risk. Additionally, changes in precipitation patterns, with more intense rainfall events and longer dry spells, can impact water availability for irrigation and human consumption. Water scarcity is already a pressing concern in the region, and climate change threatens to intensify this issue. The reliance on tourism as a significant source of revenue for Mediterranean countries is also vulnerable to climate change. High temperatures and extreme weather events can deter tourists, affecting local economies and livelihoods dependant on the sector.

Moving towards the Gulf region, we encounter another area highly susceptible to climate change impacts. With its arid climate and extensive coastline, the Gulf is at risk of experiencing more frequent and severe heatwaves, reduced freshwater availability, and coastal flooding. The Gulf region already faces some of the hottest temperatures in the world, and climate models suggest that temperature increases will be even more pronounced in this area. This extreme heat poses significant risks to human health, particularly vulnerable populations such as the elderly and those with pre-existing medical conditions. Heat-related illnesses and deaths are expected to increase if appropriate measures are not taken to mitigate the impacts of climate change.

Simultaneously, the Gulf region is grappling with dwindling freshwater resources. Prolonged droughts and over-extraction of groundwater resources have contributed to a decline in freshwater availability. Groundwater reserves are being depleted faster than they can be naturally replenished, and saltwater intrusion into freshwater aquifers is becoming a growing concern. As a response to this crisis, the United Arab Emirates (UAE) has initiated large-scale desalination projects to meet water demand. Desalination is an energy-intensive process that contributes to greenhouse gas emissions, exacerbating climate change, and exacerbating the cycle of water scarcity. Thus, it becomes essential for Gulf countries to adopt sustainable water management practises, promote water conservation, and explore alternative sources of water to address the growing water crisis.

Additionally, the climatic conditions of the Gulf region make it vulnerable to coastal flooding. Rising sea levels, coupled with more frequent and intense storm surges, threaten coastal cities and infrastructure. Cities like Dubai and Abu Dhabi, which are experiencing rapid urban development, face increased risks due to their low-lying coastal locations. Investing in resilient infrastructure, such as sea walls and elevated buildings, is crucial to protecting these vulnerable areas. Moreover, a holistic approach to coastal management that includes natural defences, such as mangrove restoration and coral reef preservation, can enhance resilience and provide additional benefits such as carbon sequestration and habitat preservation.

Turning our attention to the Indian Ocean, we witness the vulnerability of countries such as the Maldives, Seychelles, and Mauritius. Rising sea levels pose a direct threat to low-lying islands, which could potentially become uninhabitable in the future. The Maldives, for example, has an average elevation of only 1.5 metres above sea level, making it especially vulnerable to sea-level rise. Even a slight increase in sea levels can result in saltwater intrusion into freshwater resources, rendering the land unsuitable for agriculture and compromising drinking water supplies. In response to this existential threat, the Maldives has set ambitious goals to become carbon-neutral by 2030 and is investing in renewable energy projects such as solar panels and wind farms.

The Indian Ocean also experiences tropical cyclones, which are expected to become more intense and frequent with climate change. These cyclones can cause widespread destruction, damage critical infrastructure, and displace communities, particularly in coastal regions. In 2019, Cyclone Idai devastated parts of Mozambique, Zimbabwe, and Malawi, highlighting the devastating impacts of such extreme weather events. These impacts not only pose challenges for the immediate survival and livelihoods of the affected populations but also have broader implications for migration, social inequality, and national security.

In each of these regions, governments, communities, and stakeholders are recognising the urgent need for action. Efforts are being made to build climate resilience, adapt to changing conditions, and mitigate greenhouse gas emissions. International initiatives such as the Mediterranean Climate Change Initiative, the Gulf Cooperation Council for the Arab States of the Gulf, and the Indian Ocean Rim Association are facilitating collaboration and knowledge exchange among countries in these regions. Through these initiatives, countries are sharing scientific research, best practises, and technological innovations aimed at reducing greenhouse gas emissions, promoting sustainable practises, and enhancing climate resilience.

However, further investment and support are needed to scale up these initiatives and ensure they have a meaningful impact. Climate finance mechanisms such as the Green Climate Fund and the Adaptation Fund can provide financial support to these vulnerable regions to implement projects and activities that enhance resilience and promote sustainable development. The international community, including developed countries and multilateral institutions, must fulfil their commitment to providing financial resources, technology transfer, and capacity-building support to address the needs of countries most affected by climate change.

Furthermore, it is crucial to consider the social and economic implications of climate change in these areas. As sea-level rise and extreme weather events affect livelihoods and access to resources, marginalised communities are often disproportionately impacted. Vulnerable populations, including indigenous communities, women, and the economically disadvantaged, face additional barriers in adapting to and recovering from the impacts of climate change. Enhancing social protections, promoting equitable resource allocation, and empowering vulnerable populations are essential components of climate change adaptation strategies. Additionally, efforts to address climate change in these regions should incorporate the knowledge, perspectives, and traditional practises of local communities, who possess valuable insights into the ecological dynamics and sustainable resource management.

In this chapter, we have explored case studies from each of these regions, examining the specific impacts that climate change has had and the innovative responses that have been developed. We have seen examples of coastal protection measures, water management strategies, renewable energy projects, and community-based adaptation initiatives that have been implemented. By understanding the regional nuances and sharing best practises, we can inform future policy frameworks and foster greater collaboration to address the challenges of climate change in the Mediterranean, the Gulf, and the Indian Ocean. Together, we can work towards a more sustainable and resilient future for these vulnerable regions and protect the invaluable natural heritage and resources they hold. By prioritising climate action, we can strive to minimise the adverse impacts of climate change and create a more sustainable and equitable future for all.

In the Mediterranean region, countries are taking steps to mitigate and adapt to climate change. Many countries have implemented renewable energy projects, such as solar and wind farms, to reduce their reliance on fossil fuels and decrease greenhouse gas emissions. For example, Greece has invested heavily in wind energy, while Spain has become a global leader in solar energy production. Additionally, countries are implementing coastal protection measures, such as the construction of sea walls and the restoration of natural barriers like mangroves and dunes. These natural defences help to reduce the impacts of storm surges and coastal erosion.

In the Gulf region, countries are also investing in renewable energy projects and sustainable water management. The UAE, for instance, has set a target to generate 50% of its energy from renewable sources by 2050. Saudi Arabia has also announced plans to develop a $200 billion solar power project. Moreover, countries are exploring innovative water management strategies, including the use of advanced desalination technologies, water recycling, and the cultivation of salt-tolerant crops. These strategies aim to reduce the reliance on freshwater resources and promote sustainable water use.

In the Indian Ocean, countries are focusing on renewable energy and disaster preparedness. The Maldives, for example, has set a goal to generate 30% of its electricity from renewable sources by 2023 and become carbon neutral by 2030. The country has also invested in early warning systems and evacuation plans to mitigate the impacts of tropical cyclones. In Mauritius, efforts are being made to enhance coastal resilience through the protection and restoration of coral reefs, which act as natural barriers against storm surges.

At the international level, collaboration and knowledge sharing are critical in addressing the challenges posed by climate change in these regions. Regional organisations such as the Union for the Mediterranean, the Gulf Cooperation Council, and the Indian Ocean Commission play a vital role in promoting cooperation and facilitating joint initiatives. These organisations provide platforms for countries to share best practises, exchange scientific research, and develop regional strategies for climate resilience and mitigation.

Furthermore, the international community must provide financial and technical support to these vulnerable regions to implement climate change adaptation and mitigation projects. The Green Climate Fund, established under the United Nations Framework Convention on Climate Change, aims to support developing countries in their efforts to address climate change. Through financial assistance, technology transfer, and capacity building, the Green Climate Fund can enable countries in the Mediterranean, the Gulf, and the Indian Ocean to enhance their resilience and transition towards low-carbon, sustainable development.

In conclusion, the Mediterranean, the Gulf, and the Indian Ocean face significant challenges due to climate change. Rising sea levels, intense heatwaves, water scarcity, and extreme weather events threaten the ecosystems, economies, and livelihoods of these regions. However, there is hope in the form of regional cooperation, policy measures, and innovative solutions. By investing in renewable energy, sustainable water management, coastal protection, and community-based adaptation initiatives, countries in these regions can mitigate the impacts of climate change and build resilience. Additionally, international collaboration and support are essential in achieving a sustainable and resilient future for the Mediterranean, the Gulf, and the Indian Ocean. Together, we can address the unique challenges these regions face and pave the way for a more sustainable and climate-resilient future.

CLIMATE CHANGE CHALLENGES IN ARAB REGIONS

C limate change poses significant challenges to Arab regions, both in terms of its environmental impacts and the socio-economic consequences. Arab countries, which are predominantly located in arid and semi-arid regions, are already experiencing the effects of climate change, including rising temperatures, changing precipitation patterns, and increased frequency and intensity of extreme weather events.

One of the main challenges faced by Arab regions is water scarcity. These countries already face water stress due to limited freshwater resources, population growth, and increasing demands for water. Climate change exacerbates this issue by altering the hydrological cycle. Rising temperatures lead to increased evaporation rates, reducing the availability of water for agriculture, industry, and domestic use. This poses a significant threat to food security, livelihoods, and economic stability within the region. The reliance on non-renewable groundwater resources further exacerbates the challenge, as unsustainable extraction rates are likely to deplete these reserves even faster.

Furthermore, the impact of climate change on water resources in Arab regions goes beyond scarcity. It also affects water quality, with rising temperatures promoting the growth of harmful algal blooms and the spread of waterborne diseases. Changes in precipitation patterns can lead to more frequent and intense rainfall events, increasing the risk of water contamination and impairing water treatment processes. Additionally, sea-level rise and saltwater intrusion threaten freshwater supplies in coastal areas, compromising both groundwater and surface water sources. The degradation of water resources not only affects human populations but also places stress on ecosystems, which depend on these resources for their survival.

Another major challenge faced by Arab regions relates to the impact on coastal areas. Arab countries have long stretches of coastlines with many densely populated areas located along these coasts. Rising sea levels, as a result of global warming, pose a significant threat to these areas. Arab regions are particularly vulnerable to the impacts of sea-level rise due to flat topography, subsidence, and the concentration of economic activities and critical infrastructure along the coastal zones. Increased sea levels and more frequent and severe storms put these areas at risk of coastal flooding, erosion, and damage to infrastructure. This not only affects human settlements but also ecosystems and biodiversity along the coasts, which are crucial for maintaining ecological balance and providing essential ecosystem services.

Coastal ecosystems, such as mangroves, seagrass beds, and coral reefs, play a crucial role in protecting coastal areas from erosion, storm surges, and the impacts of sea-level rise. However, these ecosystems are already under significant pressure from human activities, such as coastal development, overfishing, and pollution. Climate change further compounds the threats faced by these fragile ecosystems. Rising sea temperatures contribute to coral bleaching, leading to the loss of biodiversity and the degradation of reef ecosystems. The destruction of these natural barriers not only increases the vulnerability of coastal areas to climate change impacts but also undermines the livelihoods of communities dependent on coastal resources, such as fisheries and tourism.

Furthermore, extreme heat events are becoming more common and severe in Arab regions. These high temperatures, coupled with urbanization, limited access to cooling systems, and socioeconomic disparities, increase the risks of heat-related illnesses and mortality rates. Vulnerable groups, such as the elderly, children, and outdoor workers, are particularly at risk. Moreover, extreme heat exacerbates the energy demand for cooling, further stressing the electricity infrastructure and contributing to higher carbon emissions levels.

Agriculture, a crucial sector in Arab regions, is significantly affected by climate change. Changes in precipitation patterns, including shifts in timing and intensity, coupled with increased frequency and duration of droughts, can lead to crop failures, loss of livestock, and increased desertification. Arab regions heavily rely on imports to meet their food demands, making them vulnerable to global food price volatility and supply disruptions caused by climate change impacts in other parts of the world. These climate-induced challenges in agriculture have broader implications for food security, rural livelihoods, and overall economic stability within the region.

Climate change also has implications for public health in Arab regions. It can contribute to the redistribution of infectious diseases as changing temperatures and altered precipitation patterns influence the habitats and distribution of disease vectors. Vector-borne diseases like malaria, dengue fever, and West Nile virus are of concern. Additionally, water scarcity and compromised sanitation systems due to climate change can increase the incidence of waterborne diseases. The health impacts of climate change require attention and adequate resources to mitigate and adapt to these challenges through improved public health systems and strengthened healthcare infrastructure.

Addressing these climate change challenges in Arab regions requires a multi-faceted approach that encompasses mitigation, adaptation, and resilience-building strategies. It involves policies to reduce greenhouse gas emissions, enhance resilience, and ensure adaptive capacity. Arab countries can adopt and implement mitigation measures to reduce their carbon footprints, such as promoting renewable energy sources, improving energy efficiency in sectors like buildings and industries, and implementing sustainable transportation systems. Additionally, adaptation strategies are essential to build resilience and enhance adaptive capacities in vulnerable sectors like agriculture, water management, and coastal zones. These may include measures like implementing efficient irrigation systems, promoting drought-resistant crops, improving water storage and management practices, adopting climate-smart agricultural techniques, and developing early warning systems for extreme weather events.

Regional cooperation plays a vital role in addressing climate change challenges in Arab regions. Arab countries can share knowledge, expertise, and best practices, and collaborate on regional initiatives to strengthen resilience and adapt to the changing climate collectively. The pooling of resources, joint research and development projects, capacity-building programs, and knowledge-sharing platforms can enhance climate change awareness and response strategies. Collaboration can also help in ensuring equitable outcomes for all countries and regions within the Arab League, taking into account varying vulnerabilities, capacities, and development levels.

Overall, climate change presents significant and complex challenges to Arab regions, impacting various sectors and vulnerable populations. Recognizing the urgency of the situation and the interconnectedness of climate change impacts, Arab regions must prioritize climate action and promote sustainable development to mitigate the impacts of climate change and secure a more resilient and sustainable future for their societies. By harnessing the collective knowledge, resources, and expertise within the region, Arab countries can work towards a greener and more climate-resilient future.

Previous Studies on Climate Change Effects

To understand the potential impacts of climate change on small islands and peninsulas, it is crucial to examine previous studies that have explored this topic. Numerous research papers, reports, and assessments have been conducted over the years, providing valuable insights into the effects of climate change on vulnerable regions.

One significant study that has contributed to our understanding of climate change effects is the Intergovernmental Panel on Climate Change (IPCC) assessment reports. The IPCC is a renowned scientific body established by the United Nations to provide policymakers with objective and up-to-date information on climate change. Their reports assess the scientific literature on various aspects of climate change, including its impacts, adaptation measures, and mitigation strategies.

The IPCC's assessment reports have consistently highlighted the risks and vulnerabilities faced by small islands and peninsulas due to climate change. These regions are particularly susceptible to rising sea levels, changing precipitation patterns, increased storm frequency, and intensified heatwaves. The reports have emphasised the need for urgent action to mitigate greenhouse gas emissions and implement adaptation measures to protect these vulnerable areas.

Furthermore, the IPCC's reports have also pointed out the unique characteristics of small islands and peninsulas that make them highly vulnerable to climate change impacts. For instance, the limited land area and low-lying nature of small islands make them highly susceptible to coastal erosion and flooding. This can lead to the loss of valuable terrestrial and marine ecosystems, as well as displacement of communities residing in these areas.

The IPCC's findings have been supported by numerous regional studies that have focused on the specific impacts of climate change on small islands and peninsulas. These studies have examined the social, economic, and environmental consequences of changing climate conditions. They have also investigated the adaptive capacities of local communities and the effectiveness of adaptation strategies in addressing the challenges posed by climate change.

For example, studies conducted in the Pacific Islands have revealed that the rise in sea levels threatens the livelihoods of coastal communities, as their agriculture, freshwater resources, and infrastructure become increasingly affected. Additionally, increased storm intensity and frequency pose a significant risk to these regions, leading to damage to property, loss of lives, and disruption of essential services.

Moreover, academic research and scholarly publications have made significant contributions to our understanding of climate change effects. These studies have examined various aspects, such as the ecological impacts on marine and terrestrial ecosystems, the influence of climate change on agriculture, fisheries, and food security, and the implications for human health.

Studies in coastal regions have highlighted the overwhelming evidence of ecosystem degradation due to climate change impacts. Coral reefs, vital for coastal protection and supporting biodiversity, are under threat from rising sea temperatures, ocean acidification, and coral bleaching events. Mangrove forests, which serve as natural buffers against storms and provide essential habitats, face degradation and loss due to sea level rise and increasing frequency of extreme weather events.

In addition to environmental consequences, climate change also poses significant socio-economic challenges for small islands and peninsulas. For instance, agriculture, a crucial sector for these communities, faces disruption due to changing rainfall patterns, increased salinisation of soils, and the onslaught of pests and diseases. This threatens food security, livelihoods, and the cultural identity closely tied to traditional agricultural practises.

Furthermore, the implications for human health in these regions are significant. Climate change can exacerbate existing health issues and introduce new ones through increased exposure to extreme heat, vector-borne diseases, and waterborne illnesses. Vulnerable populations, such as the elderly, children, and those with limited access to healthcare, are particularly at risk.

Case studies conducted in different regions have provided valuable insights into the specific effects of climate change on small islands and peninsulas. These case studies have examined the vulnerabilities, impacts, and adaptation strategies employed by communities facing climate change-related challenges. They have helped in identifying best practises, lessons learnt, and policy recommendations for addressing climate change effects in these regions.

By analysing and synthesising the findings from these previous studies, we can gain a comprehensive understanding of the potential effects of climate change on small islands and peninsulas. This knowledge will serve as a foundation for developing effective strategies and policies to mitigate and adapt to the impacts of climate change in these vulnerable regions.

In the following chapters, we will delve deeper into the specific impacts of climate change on small islands and peninsulas in different regional contexts, examining the socio-economic consequences, environmental implications, and policy responses. We will also explore the challenges and opportunities for building resilience in these regions and highlight innovative approaches and initiatives that have been implemented to address the effects of climate change.

Socio-Economic Impacts of Climate Change

Climate change poses significant socio-economic challenges for Arab countries, impacting various sectors and aspects of society. In this chapter, we will delve deeper into the specific impacts and explore potential solutions and strategies to mitigate and adapt to these changes.

Agriculture, as a primary economic activity in many Arab countries, is highly vulnerable to the impacts of climate change. Rising temperatures and changes in precipitation patterns affect soil moisture, crop growth, and livestock production. Arab countries already face water scarcity challenges, and climate change exacerbates this situation, straining agricultural productivity and food security.

For instance, in Egypt, one of the region's largest agricultural producers, climate change has led to longer drought periods and increased heatwaves. These adverse conditions have caused reductions in crop yields such as wheat, maise, and rice. To address these challenges, adopting sustainable agricultural practises is essential. Improved irrigation methods such as drip irrigation and precision farming technologies can optimise water usage and minimise wastage. Investing in research and innovation to develop drought-resistant crop varieties and promoting sustainable soil management techniques, such as conservation agriculture and organic farming, can enhance resilience and contribute to food security in the face of climate change.

Water resources, a critical asset for human well-being and economic development, are significantly impacted by climate change in Arab countries. Changing precipitation patterns, increased evaporation rates, and rising sea levels contribute to water scarcity, affecting both availability and quality.

Across the region, countries such as Saudi Arabia, Jordan, and Yemen face severe water scarcity challenges exacerbated by climate change.

Integrated water resource management strategies are crucial to ensure sustainable water supply while adapting to the challenges posed by climate change. These strategies encompass various aspects, including water conservation, desalination, and wastewater treatment and reuse. Implementing water-saving techniques such as water-efficient irrigation systems, rainwater harvesting, and promoting responsible water consumption habits can significantly contribute to conserving water resources. Moreover, investing in desalination technologies and utilising treated wastewater for non-potable purposes can alleviate pressure on freshwater sources. Engaging with stakeholders at all levels, including governments, communities, and businesses, and promoting awareness campaigns about water conservation are also crucial for fostering a culture of responsible water use.

The health impacts of climate change cannot be underestimated. Rising temperatures and changing weather patterns facilitate the spread of vector-borne diseases such as malaria and dengue fever. Additionally, heatwaves and extreme weather events increase the risks of heatstroke, respiratory illnesses, and mental health issues.

Countries like Iraq and Sudan have witnessed an increase in vector-borne diseases due to climate change. In response, enhancing public health systems, strengthening disease surveillance, and implementing effective vector control measures are key to reducing the health burden associated with climate change. Early warning systems can help anticipate and respond to health risks in a timely manner. Additionally, improving access to healthcare services, particularly in vulnerable communities, and strengthening healthcare infrastructure are imperative to protect the most at-risk populations. Allocating resources and training healthcare professionals in climate change-related health risks can enhance preparedness and ensure prompt responses.

Infrastructure, particularly in coastal areas, faces considerable risks from climate change. Sea-level rise, increased storm intensity, and coastal erosion can lead to flooding, damaging critical infrastructure such as roads, buildings, and harbours.

Countries like Bahrain and Qatar, with large portions of their populations residing in low-lying coastal areas, are particularly vulnerable to these risks. Retrofitting infrastructure to improve resilience, implementing coastal protection measures such as seawalls and beach nourishment, and integrating climate change considerations into infrastructure planning and design are necessary to minimise the risks posed by climate change. Innovative solutions, such as nature-based approaches that protect coastlines through the restoration of mangroves and coral reefs, can provide long-term benefits for both human settlements and ecosystems. Furthermore, incorporating climate change projections into infrastructure investment decisions can ensure that critical infrastructure is built to withstand future impacts, reducing long-term costs and minimising disruptions.

Climate change impacts also exacerbate existing socio-economic disparities, disproportionately affecting vulnerable populations. The poor, marginalised communities, and women often lack resources, knowledge, and institutional support to adapt to the changing climate effectively.

In countries like Syria and Yemen, conflicts and displacement further compound the challenges faced by vulnerable populations, making adaptation even more difficult. Ensuring equitable adaptation measures and supporting vulnerable communities through targeted policies, capacity-building initiatives, and financial assistance is essential for reducing inequalities in the face of climate change. Empowering women, who play a crucial role in climate change adaptation, is particularly important for achieving sustainable and inclusive development. Recognising the knowledge and skills of women in natural resource management, promoting women's access to education and training, and involving them in decision-making processes can enhance the effectiveness and equity of climate change adaptation efforts.

To address the socio-economic impacts of climate change in Arab countries, a multi-faceted approach is required. Policymakers should prioritise climate change adaptation and mitigation as integral components of national strategies and development plans. Strengthening regional and international cooperation is crucial for knowledge sharing, technology transfer, and resource mobilisation. Country-specific and context-specific solutions, driven by research and innovation, can contribute to building resilience and ensuring sustainable socio-economic development amidst the challenges posed by climate change.

In conclusion, the socio-economic impacts of climate change in Arab countries are far-reaching and multifaceted, affecting agriculture, water resources, human health, and infrastructure. Employing sustainable agricultural practises, improving water resource management, enhancing healthcare systems, reinforcing infrastructure resilience, and addressing socio-economic inequalities can help Arab countries adapt and mitigate the adverse impacts of climate change. Collaboration among countries and stakeholders, as well as mainstreaming climate change considerations across sectors, are essential for promoting a sustainable and resilient future in the face of climate change.

Historical Climate Data and Projections for Arab Regions

Climate change is a complex and pressing issue that requires a thorough understanding of historical climate data and projections for Arab regions. In this chapter, we will delve into the available data regarding the climate history of Arab regions and examine the projected climate changes in the coming years. By analysing this information, we can gain valuable insights into the potential impacts on the environment, ecosystems, and human communities in the Arab world.

To understand the historical climate data, it is essential to examine various sources, including meteorological records, satellite observations, and climate modelling. These sources provide a comprehensive picture of past climate patterns, enabling researchers to identify trends and anomalies. By studying long-term datasets, scientists have been able to determine the average temperature, precipitation patterns, and extreme events that have occurred in Arab regions over the past century.

Examining the historical data reveals several key trends and patterns. One notable trend is the consistent increase in temperatures across the Arab world. Over the past century, the average temperature in Arab regions has risen by approximately 1 degree Celsius. This increase is significantly higher than the global average and has significant consequences for the region's ecosystems and communities.

The rise in temperatures has led to various impacts throughout the Arab world. Heatwaves have become more frequent and intense, posing risks to human health, especially vulnerable populations such as the elderly and those with chronic illnesses. The increased temperature levels also contribute to the expansion of disease-carrying vectors, such as mosquitoes, resulting in the spread of vector-borne diseases like malaria and dengue fever.

Fertile agricultural lands have also been affected as increased temperature levels contribute to soil erosion and decreased crop productivity. Plants and crops face challenges in adapting to the changing climate, affecting yields and overall agricultural productivity. The increased occurrence of extreme weather events, such as hurricanes and dust storms, also poses threats to agricultural systems, damaging crops and infrastructure.

In addition to rising temperatures, historical data also indicates changes in precipitation patterns. Some Arab regions have experienced a decrease in rainfall, leading to droughts and water scarcity. Other areas have seen an increase in extreme rainfall events, resulting in floods and associated damages. These changes in precipitation patterns have far-reaching impacts on agriculture, water resources, and the overall socio-economic stability of Arab countries.

Droughts have become a significant concern across the Arab world, affecting food production and exacerbating water scarcity. Decreased precipitation and prolonged dry spells have led to decreased water availability for irrigation, posing challenges to the agricultural sector and threatening food security. In some regions, desertification has intensified, as dryland ecosystems struggle to cope with prolonged drought conditions.

On the other hand, regions experiencing increased rainfall events face their own set of challenges. Heavy downpours and flash floods can cause severe infrastructure damage, economic losses, and the displacement of populations. Additionally, increased precipitation may lead to waterlogging, causing soil degradation and reduced crop yields.

To supplement the historical data, climate scientists also rely on climate modelling tools to project future climate changes in Arab regions. These models consider a range of factors, including greenhouse gas emissions, ocean currents, and atmospheric circulation patterns, to simulate future climate scenarios. While these projections come with uncertainties, they provide crucial insights into potential climate trends and allow policymakers to make informed decisions.

Based on the available projections, Arab regions are expected to face several significant climate change impacts in the coming decades. These include more frequent and intense heatwaves, prolonged droughts, increased water stress, coastal flooding due to sea-level rise, and changes in agricultural productivity. These climate change effects pose substantial risks to human health, food security, and overall socio-economic development in

Arab countries.

To mitigate the impacts of climate change and build resilience in Arab regions, policymakers and stakeholders must take proactive measures. These include implementing policies and strategies to reduce greenhouse gas emissions, transitioning to clean and renewable energy sources, promoting sustainable agriculture practises, enhancing water management systems, and investing in climate adaptation and disaster risk reduction measures.

Furthermore, regional cooperation and knowledge-sharing among Arab countries are crucial to effectively tackle climate change challenges. Collaborative efforts can facilitate the exchange of best practises, scientific research, and technological advancements. This cooperation can also enable the development of joint projects and initiatives that address common climate concerns and promote sustainable development.

It is important for policymakers, researchers, and the general public to be aware of the historical climate data and projections for Arab regions. This knowledge serves as a foundation for developing effective adaptation and mitigation strategies to address climate change challenges. By utilising the available data and engaging in interdisciplinary research, Arab countries can better equip themselves to protect their ecosystems, safeguard their communities, and build resilience in the face of climate change.

In the following chapters, we will explore in-depth the socio-economic impacts of climate change in Arab regions and discuss policy responses, regional cooperation efforts, and innovative solutions. By considering the historical climate data and projections, we can develop a comprehensive understanding of the challenges and opportunities that lie ahead. Only through such comprehensive analysis and collective action can we hope to protect the future of Arab regions, promote sustainable development, and mitigate the adverse effects of climate change.

Policy Responses and Regional Cooperation

Climate change is a global challenge that requires collective action and collaboration across all levels of society and governance. In this chapter, we will delve deeper into the policy responses and regional cooperation efforts that have been implemented to address the impacts of climate change in various Arab regions.

Governments in Arab regions have recognized the urgency of addressing climate change and have made commitments to mitigate greenhouse gas emissions and adapt to the changing climate. Many countries have developed national climate change strategies and action plans based on comprehensive assessments of their vulnerabilities and capacities. These strategies outline their goals and targets for reducing emissions, promoting renewable energy, and enhancing resilience in vulnerable sectors such as agriculture, water resources, and coastal ecosystems.

For example, the United Arab Emirates (UAE), a country highly vulnerable to climate change impacts, has undertaken significant efforts to address this issue. The UAE Energy Strategy 2050 aims to increase the share of clean energy in the country's total energy mix and reduce carbon dioxide emissions by 70%. The strategy includes the development of renewable energy projects, such as solar and wind power, and the promotion of energy efficiency measures in the transportation and building sectors. The UAE's commitment to clean energy has led to the establishment of innovative projects like Masdar City, a sustainable urban development that serves as a model for low-carbon living.

Similarly, Saudi Arabia, a major global oil producer, has recognized the need to diversify its economy and reduce greenhouse gas emissions. Through its Vision 2030, the country aims to increase the share of renewable energy in the electricity sector to 50% by 2030 and implement energy efficiency measures in various sectors. Saudi Arabia has also launched the Green Saudi Initiative and the Green Middle East Initiative, which seek to expand the Kingdom's efforts in protecting the environment, preserving natural resources, and combatting pollution and climate change.

At the regional level, there have been several initiatives aimed at promoting collective action and sharing best practices. The Arab Climate Change Assessment Report is a significant effort in this regard. Led by the League of Arab States and supported by the German Development Cooperation, this report assesses the impacts and vulnerabilities of climate change in Arab countries, providing policymakers with valuable insights into the specific challenges they face. The report also offers policy recommendations for adaptation and mitigation, helping countries design and implement effective strategies tailored to their unique circumstances.

Regional cooperation is crucial in addressing climate change as it allows for the sharing of knowledge, resources, and experiences among countries facing similar challenges. The League of Arab States has established a Climate Change Unit to coordinate regional efforts, facilitate knowledge exchange, and support capacity-building initiatives. Through this unit, Arab countries work together to develop common positions and approaches in international climate negotiations, ensuring their collective interests are represented and prioritized.

The Arab Climate Resilience Initiative (ACRI) is another notable example of regional cooperation. Launched under the League of Arab States, ACRI aims to enhance the resilience of Arab countries to the impacts of climate change by fostering collaboration in areas such as water management, agriculture, and urban planning. This initiative facilitates the sharing of expertise and best practices, supporting countries in developing effective adaptation and risk reduction strategies.

In addition, the Arab region has engaged in international climate change negotiations, advocating for their interests and concerns to be addressed. Arab countries have participated in the United Nations Framework Convention on Climate Change (UNFCCC) negotiations, emphasizing the principles of common but differentiated responsibilities and respective capabilities. They have consistently highlighted the need for greater financial and technological support from developed countries to facilitate their transition to low-carbon and climate-resilient pathways.

However, despite these policy responses and regional cooperation efforts, there are still challenges that need to be addressed. One key challenge is the implementation and enforcement of climate change policies and strategies at the national level. Many countries struggle with limited financial and technical capacities, which hinder their ability to fully implement their climate change commitments. Capacity-building initiatives and international support are essential for overcoming these challenges and ensuring effective implementation of climate actions.

Furthermore, coordination and collaboration among different sectors and stakeholders are crucial for effective policy responses. This includes engaging civil society organizations, the private sector, and local communities in decision-making processes and promoting inclusive and participatory approaches. Multi-stakeholder dialogues and partnerships that involve academia, businesses, and community representatives can contribute to more holistic and locally relevant responses to climate change.

To address these challenges, innovative financing mechanisms and support from the international community are vital. Arab countries have called for increased climate finance, technology transfer, and capacity-building support to enable them to effectively implement climate change actions. This support should not only focus on mitigation efforts but also on building resilience and adaptive capacities, particularly for the most vulnerable communities.

In conclusion, addressing the impacts of climate change requires a comprehensive and multi-dimensional approach that includes policy responses at both national and regional levels. Regional cooperation plays a vital role in promoting knowledge exchange, capacity building, and shared responsibility. Arab countries have demonstrated their commitment to addressing climate change through the development of national strategies, active participation in international negotiations, and regional initiatives. However, more efforts are needed to overcome implementation challenges, secure adequate support, and ensure the effective and equitable distribution of resources and benefits among all Arab countries. By working together, the Arab regions can contribute to a more sustainable and resilient future for themselves and the planet as a whole.

Theoretical Framework: Power Structures and Environmental Justice

In this chapter, we study into the theoretical framework that underpins the analysis of power structures and environmental justice in the context of climate change. Understanding the dynamics of power and exploring the concept of environmental justice is crucial for comprehending and addressing the inequities and disparities that arise from climate change impacts.

At its core, power structures refer to the distribution and exercise of authority, control, and influence within societies. They are multi-dimensional, encompassing economic, political, social, and cultural aspects. Power shapes decision-making processes, resource allocation, and the implementation of policies, influencing who has access to resources and who is marginalised. Within the context of climate change, power structures play a pivotal role in determining who bears the burdens and benefits of environmental degradation and climate change impacts.

Environmental justice is a concept that emphasises the fair distribution of environmental risks and benefits across different social groups, taking into account issues of race, class, and gender. It recognises that vulnerable communities often bear the brunt of environmental hazards and climate change impacts, while the more powerful and privileged groups tend to have greater access to resources and protection. Environmental justice seeks to address these disparities and to ensure that all individuals and groups, regardless of their social position, have an equal voice in decision-making processes and fair access to environmental resources.

The theoretical framework we will explore draws on a range of interconnected concepts and theories, including political ecology, intersectionality, and environmental governance. Political ecology provides insights into the relationships between power, social inequality, and environmental change. It helps us understand how power is consolidated and maintained by certain groups, often at the expense of marginalised communities, leading to environmental injustices. Through the lens of political ecology, we can examine how capitalist systems, neoliberal policies, and socio-political structures contribute to environmental disparities and climate change vulnerabilities.

Intersectionality, on the other hand, highlights the multiple dimensions of identity and how different forms of oppression intersect. By examining how race, class, gender, and other social categories intersect with environmental issues, we can better understand how power structures operate and perpetuate environmental injustices. For example, low-income communities of colour may face disproportionate exposure to environmental hazards due to the intersection of race, socioeconomic status, and geographic location, leading to unequal health outcomes and limited access to resources and opportunities.

Environmental governance refers to the collective decision-making processes and institutions that shape environmental policies and management. It explores the roles of governments, non-governmental organisations, and other actors in addressing environmental challenges and ensuring just outcomes. In the context of power structures and environmental justice, studying environmental governance allows us to critically analyse how power is exercised and how different actors, with varying degrees of power and influence, shape environmental policies and practises. It helps reveal who has a voice in decision-making processes and who is excluded, thus highlighting the potential for injustices to emerge.

By applying this theoretical framework, we can thoroughly analyse how power structures shape climate change vulnerability and the distribution of resources to adapt and mitigate its impacts. We can uncover the underlying social, economic, and political factors that contribute to environmental injustice and devise strategies to address these issues. Moreover, understanding power structures and environmental justice is crucial for designing effective policy responses and promoting inclusive and sustainable solutions. It sheds light on the need for participatory approaches, inclusive decision-making, and the empowerment of marginalised communities to effectively confront climate change challenges.

In the following chapters, we will apply this theoretical framework to our case studies in the Mediterranean, the Gulf, and the Indian Ocean regions. By examining the power dynamics and environmental justice issues specific to these regions, we aim to deepen our understanding of climate change impacts and identify opportunities for more equitable and just responses. The insights gained from these case studies will contribute to the development of practical strategies and policies that strive for environmental justice and sustainability at both the local and global levels.

Remember, the theoretical framework presented in this chapter serves as a lens through which we can critically analyse the complexities of power structures and environmental justice in the context of climate change. It offers a conceptual framework for understanding the underlying dynamics and striving towards more equitable and sustainable outcomes. Through an in-depth examination of these concepts, we can better grasp the intricacies of power structures and their influence on environmental justice, ultimately working towards a more just and sustainable future.

Conflict, Migration, and Adaptation

As the effects of climate change become increasingly prominent, they intersect with existing social and political dynamics, often exacerbating tensions and conflicts. This chapter delves into the complex relationship between climate change, conflict, migration, and the adaptive strategies employed by communities in response to these challenges.

Climate change has the potential to act as a threat multiplier, exacerbating existing tensions and conflicts in susceptible regions. Scarce resources, such as water and arable land, can become even scarcer as climate change disrupts traditional patterns of precipitation and agriculture. This can heighten competition and trigger conflicts over these resources, leading to tensions between different communities, ethnic groups, or even nations.

For example, in the Sahel region of Africa, climate change-induced droughts have intensified competition over dwindling water resources and fertile land. This has pitted nomadic herders against sedentary farmers, escalating conflicts between different ethnic groups and exacerbating social divisions. These conflicts are often rooted in historical grievances, but resource scarcity acts as a catalyst, fuelling the tensions and making resolution more challenging.

Similarly, in parts of South Asia, the melting of glaciers and changing rainfall patterns have caused water scarcity, impacting agricultural productivity. This has led to disputes over water-sharing between upstream and downstream communities, and in some cases, it has even strained diplomatic relations between countries. The vulnerable position of small island nations, like the Maldives and Tuvalu, also highlights the threats they face from rising sea levels, pushing them towards future conflicts and forced migration.

Furthermore, climate change-induced natural disasters, such as floods, hurricanes, and droughts, can displace entire populations, creating a wave of climate refugees. Migration becomes a strategy for survival as communities are forced to leave their homes in search of better living conditions. This mass movement of people can strain host communities and exacerbate existing social, political, and economic vulnerabilities, often leading to social unrest and conflict.

In the Pacific region, for instance, the increased frequency and intensity of tropical storms and rising sea levels have forced communities to relocate. In some cases, these relocations have become sources of conflict as host communities struggle to accommodate the influx of displaced persons, resulting in strained resources, competition, and tensions. The vulnerable communities of Bangladesh also face the dual challenge of cyclones and sea-level rise, which contribute to their high rates of climate-induced migration, making them prone to conflicts over limited resources.

Adaptation to these changing environmental conditions is crucial for communities affected by climate change. However, the capacity to adapt varies greatly among different regions and social groups. Vulnerable communities, particularly those with limited resources and marginalised populations, face significant challenges in adapting to the impacts of climate change and the associated conflicts and migrations.

Successful adaptation strategies involve both community-based and policy-driven approaches. Community-based adaptation focuses on empowering local communities to build resilience, enhance their livelihoods, and reduce vulnerabilities. This can include measures such as diversification of livelihoods, sustainable natural resource management, and the strengthening of social networks.

For instance, in the Nigre Delta region of Nigeria, community-based adaptation initiatives have involved developing alternative livelihoods, such as fish farming and eco-tourism, to reduce dependence on oil extraction and protect the fragile coastal ecosystem. Similarly, in the mountainous regions of Nepal, communities have adopted collective farming practises, water conservation techniques, and early warning systems for weather-related disasters to adapt to changing climatic conditions.

Policy-driven adaptation, on the other hand, requires governmental and international efforts to create a supportive environment for adaptation activities. This involves policies and measures that prioritise vulnerable communities, provide access to resources and technologies, and ensure the protection of human rights and social justice. It also involves addressing the root causes of conflicts and tensions, promoting peacebuilding, and fostering cooperation among different communities and nations.

For instance, the United Nations Framework Convention on Climate Change (UNFCCC) has emphasised the importance of adaptive measures that address the needs of vulnerable communities, highlighting the principle of common but differentiated responsibilities. The Green Climate Fund, established under the UNFCCC, aims to support adaptation efforts and provide financial resources to communities in need.

In addition to community-based and policy-driven approaches, technological innovations play a crucial role in climate change adaptation. Advancements in renewable energy technologies, such as solar and wind power, provide opportunities for communities to transition away from fossil fuel dependence, reducing greenhouse gas emissions and building resilience to future climate impacts. Furthermore, innovations in climate-smart agriculture and water management techniques can help communities optimise resource use and agricultural productivity, making them more resilient to climate change.

Education and information dissemination also play a vital role in climate change adaptation. Increasing awareness and understanding of climate change risks, adaptation strategies, and the interconnectedness of communities can empower individuals and communities to take proactive measures. Education systems, media platforms, and community outreach programmes can facilitate knowledge exchange and capacity building, enabling communities to make informed decisions and take appropriate actions.

In conclusion, climate change not only poses direct environmental challenges but also amplifies existing conflicts and triggers migration as communities struggle to adapt. Understanding the complex interplay between climate change, conflict, migration, and adaptation is essential for developing effective policies and strategies to mitigate the impacts and ensure the well-being and resilience of vulnerable communities. Only through a comprehensive and integrated approach, involving community-based efforts, policy-driven initiatives, technological innovations, and education, can we address the intertwined challenges and foster a sustainable and just future for all.

COMMUNITY RESILIENCE AND ADAPTATION

I n the face of climate change, communities around the world are experiencing the impact of extreme weather events, rising sea levels, and changing environmental conditions. This chapter explores the concept of community resilience and adaptation, focusing on how communities can effectively respond and adapt to the challenges posed by climate change. By building resilience and implementing adaptive strategies, communities can better withstand the adverse effects of climate change and thrive in a changing world.

Understanding Community Resilience:

Community resilience refers to the ability of a community to bounce back and recover from the impacts of climate change. It involves the capacity to anticipate, cope with, and adapt to adverse conditions, while continuing to function and meet the needs of its members. Resilient communities are better equipped to withstand and recover from natural disasters, extreme weather events, and other climate-related challenges.

Factors Influencing Community Resilience:

Several factors contribute to community resilience and affect its ability to adapt to climate change. These include social networks and relationships, availability of resources, access to information and technology, governance structures, cultural beliefs and practices, physical infrastructure within the community, and policies and institutions in place to support adaptation efforts. Building resilience requires addressing these factors in a coordinated and holistic manner.

1. Social Networks and Relationships:

Strong social networks and relationships form the foundation for community resilience. When individuals within a community have close ties and trust each other, they are more likely to work together during times of crisis. Social cohesion aids in information sharing, collaborative decision-making, and resource pooling. Building and nurturing social networks through community organizing, support groups, and collective activities strengthens resilience. It is important to create spaces for dialogue and participation, enabling community members to actively contribute to decision-making processes and collectively shape their future.

2. Availability of Resources:

Access to resources is essential for communities to adapt to climate change. These resources may include financial capital, natural resources, technology, infrastructure, healthcare services, and education. Resilient communities ensure that these resources are accessible to all members, particularly the most vulnerable. Collaborative efforts between governments, NGOs, and community-based organizations are needed to ensure equitable distribution of resources. It is crucial to prioritize the needs and voices of marginalized groups, ensuring nobody is left behind.

3. Access to Information and Technology:

Access to accurate and timely information is crucial for effective decision-making and adaptation. Communities need climate data, early warning systems, and information on available resources and adaptation strategies. Governments and organizations should prioritize providing communities with accessible, understandable, and context-specific information. Utilizing technology, such as mobile apps, community radio, or internet platforms, can help bridge the information gap. Enhancing digital literacy within communities can empower individuals to access and use information to make informed decisions.

4. Governance Structures:

Effective governance structures ensure that communities have the necessary support and resources to adapt to climate change. Transparent and participatory decision-making processes that involve community members in planning and policy formulation foster resilience. Good governance practices support the creation of enabling environments, where trust, accountability, and inclusive decision-making systems are established. Strengthening local capacities for self-governance, including training community leaders and fostering collaboration between different sectors, can enhance community resilience.

5. Cultural Beliefs and Practices:

Cultural beliefs and practices often shape community responses to environmental changes. Indigenous knowledge, traditional practices, and local wisdom hold valuable insights on how to adapt to climate change. Incorporating and integrating this knowledge into community planning and decision-making processes can enhance resilience and foster sustainable solutions. Communities can also leverage cultural identities to build collective resilience and stewardship of natural resources. Recognizing and respecting diverse cultural perspectives is crucial for localized and context-specific adaptation strategies.

6. Physical Infrastructure:

Investing in resilient infrastructure is crucial for communities to withstand climate-related hazards. This includes building or retrofitting structures to withstand strong winds, floods, and other extreme weather events. Designing infrastructure to adapt to changing climate conditions, such as sustainable drainage systems, green infrastructure, and coastal protection measures, can promote resilience and reduce vulnerability. Incorporating nature-based solutions, such as wetlands restoration and urban green spaces, can also provide multiple benefits including carbon sequestration, biodiversity protection, and improved well-being of community members.

7. Diversifying Livelihoods:

Overdependence on a single livelihood can make a community vulnerable to climate change impacts. Encouraging diversification of livelihood options can enhance community resilience. Promoting sustainable agriculture, supporting small-scale entrepreneurship, and developing alternative sources of income can create a safety net against climate-related shocks. Building capacity and providing training in new skills enable community members to adapt to changing economic opportunities. Engaging youth and women in sustainable livelihoods can bring fresh perspectives and strengthen the resilience of the entire community.

8. Policies and Institutions:

Supportive policies and institutions play a crucial role in enabling community resilience and adaptation. Governments need to develop and implement climate change adaptation plans that address the needs and priorities of communities. These plans should incorporate community input, establish clear targets, and provide adequate resources to implement adaptation measures. Effective policies also create incentives for innovative solutions, encourage collaboration between different actors, and provide legal frameworks to safeguard the rights and interests of vulnerable communities.

Conclusion:

Community resilience and adaptation are key components of climate change response. By fostering strong social networks, diversifying livelihoods, strengthening infrastructure, promoting local knowledge, facilitating access to information, strengthening governance structures, and building capacity, communities can enhance their ability to cope with climate change impacts. Building resilience is a continuous process that requires collaboration, participation, and long-term commitment from stakeholders at all levels. Empowering communities to adapt and thrive in the face of climate change is essential for a sustainable and resilient future. Through collective action and shared responsibilities, communities can inspire global transformation and create a world that embraces change while preserving the well-being of both people and the planet.

SOCIAL CAPITAL AND CLIMATE CHANGE AWARENESS

I n this chapter, we will explore the concept of social capital and its relevance to climate change awareness and response. Social capital refers to the resources embedded within social networks, including trust, norms, and social connections, that enable individuals and communities to cooperate and work together towards common goals. As our world grapples with the challenges posed by climate change, understanding the role of social capital becomes crucial in fostering awareness and effective responses.

The Importance of Social Capital:

Social capital plays a significant role in climate change awareness for several reasons. Firstly, social networks facilitate the exchange of knowledge, information, and experiences, thereby enhancing collective understanding of climate change impacts and adaptation strategies.

Through these networks, individuals can access information about climate change science, its potential consequences, and the best practices for mitigation and adaptation. Effective communication and information sharing within social networks not only increase awareness but also empower individuals with the knowledge to make informed decisions and take action.

Moreover, social capital enhances the adaptive capacity of communities by fostering innovation and learning through shared experiences. By drawing upon the collective wisdom and experiences of individuals within a network, communities can develop adaptive strategies that are contextually relevant and effective.

This adaptive capacity is crucial in addressing the diverse and complex challenges associated with climate change, such as extreme weather events, sea-level rise, and shifts in ecosystems. Networks can serve as platforms for sharing lessons learned, showcasing successful initiatives, and disseminating innovative approaches to climate change adaptation and mitigation across communities.

Secondly, social capital promotes collaboration and collective action. In the face of climate change, unified efforts are essential to address the wide-ranging impacts on communities, ecosystems, and economies. By fostering trust and cooperation through social networks, individuals are more likely to work together towards common goals, such as reducing greenhouse gas emissions, implementing sustainable practices, and developing resilient communities.

Within social networks, individuals can pool resources, share costs, and coordinate action, leading to more efficient and impactful responses to climate change. Collective action can take various forms, ranging from community-led projects such as renewable energy installations and climate-smart agriculture to advocacy and policy initiatives that drive systemic change at regional or global scales.

Furthermore, social capital can serve as a catalyst for innovative solutions. By facilitating cross-sector collaborations and the exchange of ideas, social networks have the potential to spark creative approaches to address climate change challenges. This can include community-led initiatives, grassroots movements, and public-private partnerships that leverage the strengths and resources of diverse stakeholders.

Factors Influencing Social Capital and Climate Change Awareness:

Various factors influence the development of social capital and climate change awareness within communities. Understanding these factors is essential in designing effective strategies to foster social capital and enhance climate change awareness. Some of the key factors include:

1. Connectivity: The level of interconnectedness and communication within a community affects the strength and effectiveness of social networks. Strong social ties and regular interactions foster trust, cooperation, and the dissemination of climate change information.

In the context of climate change, technological advancements offer new opportunities for connectivity. Online platforms, social media, and virtual communities provide spaces where individuals can connect, share knowledge, and collaborate despite geographical barriers. These digital networks have the potential to amplify climate change awareness and mobilize actions globally.

However, it is crucial to acknowledge the digital divide, where marginalized communities may have limited access to technology and, consequently, reduced opportunities for connectivity. Bridging this divide through inclusive policies and initiatives is key to ensuring equitable access to social capital and climate change awareness.

2. Cultural and Social Norms: The cultural and social norms prevalent within a community can shape climate change awareness and response. Communities that prioritize collective well-being, environmental stewardship, and cooperation are more likely to have higher levels of social capital related to climate change.

Cultural norms can influence how individuals perceive and respond to climate change. For example, communities deeply rooted in indigenous or traditional knowledge systems may have inherent resilience strategies and adaptation practices already embedded in their cultural practices. Recognizing and respecting these cultural norms and integrating them into climate change responses can lead to more effective and sustainable outcomes.

Additionally, social norms play a role in facilitating or inhibiting climate change awareness. Social pressure, societal expectations, and collective values can either encourage or hinder behavioral changes necessary for climate change mitigation and adaptation. By aligning climate action with existing cultural and social norms, communities can harness social capital to drive sustainable change.

3. Leadership and Governance: Effective leadership and supportive governance structures can nurture social capital by encouraging participation, facilitating communication, and promoting collaboration. Local leaders have a vital role in advocating for climate change awareness and mobilizing

community efforts.

Leadership that is grounded in empathy, inclusivity, and long-term vision creates an enabling environment for social capital to thrive. Such leaders bridge divides, bring together diverse stakeholders, and empower communities to take ownership of climate change issues. They facilitate dialogues, create platforms for collaboration, and ensure that decision-making processes are accountable, transparent, and participatory.

Communities can also build collective leadership, where multiple individuals or groups take on leadership roles based on their expertise and interests. Distributed leadership models ensure that the pool of knowledge, ideas, and resources is maximized, leading to more resilient and sustainable outcomes.

4. Inequality and Social Justice: Inequality and social justice issues may impact the distribution of social capital and climate change awareness. Marginalized and vulnerable communities often have limited access to resources and information, hindering their capacity to respond effectively to climate change impacts. Addressing these inequalities is crucial to ensure inclusive and equitable climate change awareness.

Disproportionate vulnerability to climate change is often linked to existing social, economic, and political inequalities. Low-income communities, indigenous peoples, women, and minority groups are frequently at the forefront of climate change impacts due to historic and systemic injustices.

Acknowledging and confronting these inequalities through targeted interventions and policies is crucial in building social capital and fostering climate change awareness. This can include initiatives aimed at enhancing access to resources, empowering marginalized communities, and creating inclusive decision-making processes that value diverse perspectives.

Promoting Social Capital and Climate Change Awareness:

To enhance social capital and climate change awareness, concerted efforts are required from various stakeholders. These efforts should include:

1. Building Social Networks: Facilitating the formation and strengthening of social networks is vital in promoting climate change awareness. This can be achieved through community engagement initiatives, educational programs, and the establishment of platforms that foster information exchange and collaboration.

Building social networks should consider the diversity of stakeholders, ensuring that they include individuals, community organizations, academic institutions, businesses, and government agencies. Encouraging collaboration and active participation from these diverse groups not only enhances climate change awareness but also fosters collective ownership and responsibility for climate change actions.

2. Empowering Local Leaders: Supporting and empowering local leaders is instrumental in mobilizing communities and facilitating climate change awareness. Providing resources, training, and platforms for leadership can help foster social capital and enhance community resilience in the face of climate change.

Capacity-building programs and mentorship opportunities can empower individuals to take on leadership roles and inspire others within their communities. By investing in education and training, individuals can gain skills and knowledge necessary for climate change awareness and adaptation. Furthermore, platforms such as community-based organizations and local chambers of commerce can serve as hubs for local leadership development and fostering social capital.

3. Communication and Education: Effective communication strategies, including targeted educational campaigns, can increase climate change awareness and knowledge. Communicating the science, impact sand urgency of climate change in accessible and engaging ways is crucial in mobilizing public support and action.

Climate change education should be integrated into school curricula at all levels, promoting understanding of the causes, consequences, and solutions to climate change. It should also emphasize the importance of individual and collective actions in addressing climate change.

Moreover, communication efforts should take into account cultural and linguistic diversity, ensuring that messages are tailored to resonate with different communities. Utilizing diverse mediums, such as storytelling, visual media, and community events, can effectively convey climate change messages and foster climate change awareness.

4. Collaboration and Partnerships: Collaboration among stakeholders is essential for building social capital and fostering climate change awareness. By creating partnerships across sectors, including government agencies, non-profit organizations, businesses, and academia, communities can leverage diverse expertise, resources, and networks.

Collaborative initiatives can involve joint research projects, sharing best practices, and implementing climate change mitigation and adaptation measures. Public-private partnerships can also drive innovation and spur investment in climate-friendly technologies and practices.

Additionally, collaboration should extend beyond local boundaries and engage regional, national, and international networks. By connecting communities and sharing experiences, knowledge, and resources, global collaboration can accelerate climate change awareness and action.

5. Addressing Inequalities: Addressing equity and social justice issues is critical in building social capital and fostering climate change awareness. Efforts to promote climate change awareness should prioritize marginalized and vulnerable communities, ensuring that they have access to resources, information, and decision-making processes.

Engaging with community leaders, grassroots organizations, and community-based solutions can help address specific challenges faced by marginalized communities. By amplifying their voices and incorporating their perspectives, climate change actions can be more inclusive, effective, and sustainable.

Equity-centered approaches should also be integrated into policy-making and governance structures. Ensuring that climate change policies and actions prioritize the needs and concerns of all communities, particularly those most impacted, can contribute to building social capital and fostering climate change awareness.

Conclusion:

Social capital plays a vital role in climate change awareness and response. By fostering knowledge exchange, trust, and cooperation, social networks enable individuals and communities to understand the challenges posed by climate change and develop effective strategies for mitigation and adaptation.

Understanding the factors that influence the development of social capital, such as connectivity, cultural norms, leadership and governance, and inequality, is essential in designing strategies to promote social capital and enhance climate change awareness.

Efforts to promote social capital and climate change awareness should focus on building social networks, empowering local leaders, improving communication and education, fostering collaboration and partnerships, and addressing inequalities.

By leveraging social capital and fostering climate change awareness, communities can be better equipped to tackle the challenges of climate change and build a sustainable and resilient future.

Case Study Selection

In order to delve deeper into understanding the impacts of climate change in Arab regions, it is crucial to conduct case studies that shed light on specific instances and their unique challenges. This chapter aims to outline the process and criteria behind the selection of case studies for further analysis, ensuring a comprehensive examination of the diverse regions affected by climate change.

Purpose of Case Study Selection:

The purpose of conducting case studies is to examine real-life scenarios in detail, allowing for a nuanced analysis of the interplay between climate change and regional dynamics. Through careful selection, these case studies will contribute to a better understanding of the socio-economic impacts, adaptation strategies, and policy responses in the face of climate change in Arab regions.

Selection Criteria:

1. Geographic Representation:

To ensure a comprehensive understanding of the impacts of climate change in Arab regions, case studies will be selected to represent a range of geographic locations. These may include regions in the Mediterranean, such as Egypt, Tunisia, Morocco, Algeria, and Lebanon, which are witnessing increased water scarcity, rising temperatures, and changing rainfall patterns. Additionally, case studies will be selected from Gulf countries like Saudi Arabia, Kuwait, Qatar, and the United Arab Emirates, where extreme heat and sea-level rise affect coastal communities and oil-dependent economies. Indian Ocean islands like Comoros and Maldives, prone to sea-level rise and extreme weather events, will also be considered. By encompassing diverse geographical areas, the study ensures a comprehensive representation of the challenges and responses across the spectrum.

2. Vulnerability:

A key criterion for case study selection is the vulnerability of the region or community to climate change impacts. Regions with high vulnerability, such as small islands, coastal areas, or densely populated urban centers, will be given priority. For example, the case study on the Maldives will shed light on the unique challenges faced by a small island nation at risk of submersion due to sea-level rise. In contrast, the case study on Cairo, Egypt, will examine the impacts of climate change on densely populated urban areas prone to water scarcity and extreme heat events. Another case study could focus on the vulnerability of the agricultural sector in Algeria, which is highly dependent on rainfall patterns and subject to desertification. By studying vulnerable regions, the project aims to identify the unique challenges they face and the adaptation measures employed.

3. Sectoral Impacts:

Case studies will also be selected to cover a broad range of sectoral impacts, including agriculture, water resources, tourism, infrastructure, and energy. The case study on agriculture in Tunisia, for example, will explore the impact of changing rainfall patterns and increasing temperatures on crop yields and food security. The case study on water resources in Saudi Arabia will examine the challenges posed by increasing water scarcity and the strategies implemented to manage water supplies, including desalination. Another case study may focus on the tourism sector in Oman, investigating the effects of rising temperatures on coastal ecosystems and the subsequent impacts on the tourism industry. Additionally, a case study on renewable energy in the United Arab Emirates could shed light on their efforts to transition to a low-carbon economy. This approach allows for a holistic analysis of the effects of climate change on various sectors and the subsequent implications for the overall socio-economic well-being of the communities involved.

4. Diverse Socio-Political Contexts:

To capture the complexity of climate change impacts, case studies will be selected to represent a variety of socio-political contexts within Arab regions. These may include countries with different governance structures, levels of economic development, or cultural backgrounds. For instance, a case study on Morocco will examine the country's climate change policies, which combine traditional knowledge and modern technology to promote sustainable development. In contrast, a case study on Kuwait may explore the challenges faced by an oil-dependent economy in transitioning to a low-carbon future. Another case study could focus on Lebanon, where the effects of climate change are compounded by political and social instability. This approach ensures a comprehensive analysis that considers the influence of different contexts on adaptation strategies.

5. Existing Research and Data Availability:

Another crucial criterion for case study selection is the availability of sufficient research and data. To ensure reliable and robust analysis, case studies will be chosen based on the availability of extensive research and data resources. This includes scientific literature, government reports, and ground-level surveys conducted by relevant organizations. Researchers will collaborate with local partners and stakeholders to ensure the collection of accurate and up-to-date data. This approach ensures that the selected case studies can provide valuable insights into the impacts, responses, and outcomes related to climate change. Additionally, it enables the identification of data gaps, stimulating further research efforts to improve our understanding of climate change impacts in these regions.

Conclusion:

The selection of case studies is a critical step in conducting a comprehensive analysis of the impacts and responses to climate change in Arab regions. By considering geographic representation, vulnerability, sectoral impacts, socio-political contexts, and data availability, this research aims to provide a holistic understanding of the diverse challenges and adaptation strategies evident across different regions. The subsequent chapters will explore the selected case studies in detail, offering insights and lessons learned for policymakers, practitioners, and the general public. These in-depth case studies, facilitated by extensive research and data availability, will contribute to our collective understanding of climate change impacts, enabling more effective adaptation measures and policies to address the unique challenges faced by Arab regions.

DATA COLLECTION METHODS

To accurately and reliably gather data on climate change impacts, it is crucial to employ appropriate methods of data collection. The selection of data collection methods may vary based on research objectives, geographical region of study, and availability of resources. This chapter provides an in-depth overview of various data collection methods commonly used in climate change research, highlighting their potential advantages and limitations.

1. Remote Sensing:

Remote sensing techniques utilise satellite imagery and other remote sensing instruments to collect data on various environmental variables. This method allows researchers to monitor changes in land cover, temperature, precipitation, and other climatic factors over large spatial and temporal scales. Remote sensing plays a crucial role in analysing the Earth's atmosphere, oceans, and surface, providing valuable insights into the dynamics of climate change. It is particularly useful in regions where ground-based data collection is limited or challenging.

Remote sensing operates based on different principles such as passive remote sensing, which measures the radiation naturally emitted by Earth's surface and the atmosphere, or active remote sensing, which sends out pulses of energy and measures the reflected or backscattered signals. Passive sensors, like those measuring visible and infrared radiation, can provide detailed information about the Earth's surface composition, vegetation health, and cloud cover. Active sensors, such as radar and lidar systems, can penetrate clouds and provide information about surface elevation, sea ice thickness, and forest structure.

However, it is important to consider the limitations of remote sensing, such as cloud cover obstructing satellite imagery and potential errors in data interpretation due to calibration issues. Additionally, the availability of certain data products may be limited or require a subscription, making it less accessible for some researchers. Moreover, interpreting remote sensing data may require specialised skills and expertise.

2. Ground-based Monitoring:

Ground-based monitoring involves the installation of sensors and instruments at specific sites to track climate parameters directly. This method provides high-resolution data, which can be tailored to specific research needs. Ground-based monitoring stations can measure temperature, humidity, wind speed, rainfall, greenhouse gas concentrations, and other relevant variables. Regular maintenance and calibration of instruments are essential to ensure data accuracy.

Ground-based monitoring networks, such as meteorological stations and air quality monitoring stations, provide continuous real-time data, allowing for the detection of short-term climate variations and extreme weather events. These networks are often operated by national meteorological agencies or research institutions. Ground-based monitoring is especially valuable for monitoring localised climate conditions, studying short-term variations, and validating remote sensing data.

However, the coverage area of ground-based monitoring is limited, making it less suitable for capturing data on a large regional or global scale. Maintaining a network of monitoring stations can be resource-intensive, requiring funding and dedicated personnel. Furthermore, the locations of monitoring stations should be carefully selected to ensure representativeness of the area under study.

3. Surveys and Questionnaires:

Surveys and questionnaires are powerful tools for collecting socio-economic data related to climate change impacts. These methods involve interviewing individuals or distributing questionnaires to gather information on attitudes, perceptions, behaviours, and adaptation strategies. Surveys can provide valuable insights into the impacts of climate change on communities, households, and individuals, as well as their capacity for adaptation and mitigation.

Well-designed surveys allow for quantitative analysis and statistical inference, contributing to robust findings. They can be conducted through various methods, such as face-to-face interviews, telephone interviews, online surveys, and mail surveys. Surveys can cover a wide range of topics, including climate-related hazards, changes in natural resource availability, livelihood impacts, and perception of climate policies.

Care should be taken to ensure the representativeness and reliability of survey samples to avoid biases. Random sampling techniques can help achieve a representative sample, but it is essential to account for potential biases in response rates and non-response. Consideration of cultural, language, and accessibility factors is also crucial to ensure inclusivity and reach diverse populations. Additionally, survey questions should be clear, unambiguous, and appropriate for the target audience.

4. Interviews and Focus Groups:

In-depth interviews and focus groups enable researchers to gather qualitative data on climate change impacts and adaptation. These methods involve engaging with key stakeholders, such as community members, policymakers, and experts, to understand their experiences, perspectives, and knowledge of climate change. Interviews provide an opportunity to explore individual experiences, understand decision-making processes, and obtain detailed information about specific contexts.

Focus groups involve bringing together a small group of individuals to engage in interactive discussions facilitated by a moderator. This method allows for the exploration of shared experiences, group dynamics, and the emergence of collective knowledge. It is particularly useful for capturing diverse perspectives and uncovering consensus or dissent regarding climate change impacts and adaptation strategies.

Interviews and focus groups provide rich and contextual information that complements quantitative data, offering deeper insights into the social, economic, and cultural dimensions of climate change. By allowing participants to share their knowledge and experiences, these methods enable researchers to uncover unique regional or community-specific challenges and solutions. However, conducting interviews and focus groups can be time-consuming, and it requires skilled interviewers or moderators to facilitate open and meaningful discussions while maintaining data validity.

5. Case Studies:

Case studies involve in-depth investigations of specific regions or communities to understand the localised impacts of climate change. This method combines various data collection techniques, such as interviews, surveys, observations, and document analysis, to gain a comprehensive understanding of the complex interactions between climate change and socio-economic factors. Case studies provide detailed and context-specific data, allowing researchers to identify unique challenges, vulnerabilities, and potential adaptive responses.

Case studies are particularly valuable when studying complex systems and when other methods may not capture the intricacies of a specific case. They shed light on the social, environmental, and economic dimensions of climate change impacts, contributing to a nuanced understanding. The findings from case studies may not be easily generalisable to larger populations or different geographical regions due to their specificity. However, they can provide valuable insights and generate hypotheses for further investigation.

Selection of case study sites should consider geographical, socio-economic, and climatic diversity to ensure a comprehensive understanding of climate change impacts. Researchers should also be mindful of ethical considerations, such as informed consent and confidentiality, when collecting data through interviews, observations, or document analysis.

6. Review of Existing Data:
Reviewing existing data is an essential initial step in climate change research. It involves analysing publicly available data from government agencies, research institutions, and international organisations. By examining historical climate records, socio-economic indicators, and policy documents, researchers can identify trends, patterns, and gaps in existing knowledge.

This method allows for the synthesis and integration of diverse data sources, providing a broader understanding of climate change impacts. It also facilitates the assessment of long-term changes and enables comparisons across regions or countries. Existing data sources include climate model outputs, climate reanalysis products, socio-economic databases, land use/land cover datasets, and historical climate observations.

However, the quality and reliability of existing data should be carefully assessed. Inconsistencies or gaps in data may arise due to differences in measurement techniques, changes in data collection methods over time, or limited availability of data from certain regions or time periods. Data quality control procedures, verification, and homogenisation techniques can help ensure the reliability and accuracy of the data used in research.

Conclusion:

Selecting appropriate data collection methods is fundamental to ensuring the validity and reliability of climate change research. A comprehensive approach that utilises multiple data collection methods, including ground-based monitoring, remote sensing, surveys and questionnaires, interviews and focus groups, and case studies, can provide a holistic understanding of climate change impacts and adaptation strategies. Each method has its own advantages and limitations, and researchers should carefully consider their research objectives, resources, and the characteristics of the study area when choosing the most suitable methods.

Remote sensing is particularly useful for monitoring large-scale changes in land cover and climate variables. It provides extensive coverage and allows for the analysis of long-term trends. Ground-based monitoring, on the other hand, provides high-resolution data that is essential for understanding localised climate conditions and short-term variations. It is particularly valuable for validating remote sensing data and detecting extreme weather events.

Surveys and questionnaires are powerful tools for gathering socio-economic data and capturing the perceptions and behaviours of individuals and communities. They provide quantitative data that can be analysed statistically, contributing to robust findings. Interviews and focus groups, on the other hand, offer qualitative insights, allowing researchers to dive deeper into individual experiences, decision-making processes, and collective knowledge.

Case studies provide in-depth analysis of specific regions or communities, allowing for the identification of unique challenges, vulnerabilities, and adaptive responses. They provide context-specific data and contribute to a nuanced understanding of the impacts of climate change. Reviewing existing data is also crucial as it allows for the synthesis of diverse sources and the identification of trends and gaps in knowledge.

It is important to note that no single data collection method can provide a complete picture of climate change impacts. A combination of methods that complement each other can provide a more comprehensive and robust understanding. Additionally, researchers should consider the strengths and limitations of each method, as well as ethical considerations, when designing their data collection approach.

By employing appropriate data collection methods, researchers can gather accurate and reliable data on climate change impacts and adaptation strategies. This data is essential for informing policy decisions, developing effective adaptation measures, and mitigating the negative effects of climate change.

Quantitative Analysis of Climate Data

I n order to comprehensively understand the impacts and implications of climate change, it is crucial to undertake a quantitative analysis of climate data. This chapter aims to provide an in-depth overview of the methods and techniques used in this analysis, highlighting the importance of data collection, processing, and interpretation. By employing rigorous scientific methods, we can obtain valuable insights into the current and future climate scenarios, allowing for informed decision-making and policy formulation.

Data Collection:

The first step in the quantitative analysis of climate data is the collection of reliable and accurate data. This involves the use of various sources such as meteorological stations, satellite imagery, remote sensing, and climate models. Meteorological stations provide ground-based measurements of temperature, rainfall, wind patterns, pressure, humidity, solar radiation, and other atmospheric variables. However, it is necessary to consider data biases arising from factors such as urban heat island effects, changes in station locations or instrumentation over time, and inconsistent measurement protocols. Quality control procedures are applied to identify and rectify errors, outliers, and inconsistencies in the data.

Satellite imagery provides a broader perspective by capturing information on a larger spatial scale, including sea surface temperature, cloud cover, land surface temperature, vegetation indices, and aerosol concentrations. Remote sensing techniques, including LIDAR and radar, offer additional information on the vertical structure of the atmosphere and surface characteristics. While satellite data provides valuable information, it also requires calibration and validation to ensure accuracy and reliability.

Climate models, based on mathematical formulas representing the physical, chemical, and biological processes that influence the climate system, simulate climate patterns and help predict future scenarios. These models combine data from different sources and help fill gaps in observational data. However, it is important to acknowledge that climate models have limitations and uncertainties associated with various factors, such as the representation of complex processes, parameterizations, and uncertainties in future emissions scenarios.

Data Processing:
Once the data is collected, it needs to be processed to ensure consistency and compatibility. This includes quality control checks to identify and rectify any errors or inconsistencies in the data. Various statistical techniques, such as outlier detection, data smoothing, and data transformations, can be employed to preprocess the data and remove any biases. Outliers are data points that deviate significantly from the general pattern and may arise due to measurement errors or extreme events. Data smoothing techniques,

such as moving averages or low-pass filters, can help eliminate short-term fluctuations and highlight long-term trends. Data transformations, such as logarithmic or exponential transformations, can be used to normalize skewed data distributions.

Spatial and temporal interpolation techniques can help fill in missing data points and create a continuous dataset. Spatial interpolation methods, such as kriging or inverse distance weighting, estimate values at unsampled locations based on the spatial relationship between neighboring observations. Temporal interpolation techniques, such as linear interpolation or cubic splines, estimate values at missing time points. Additionally, data homogenization procedures can be applied to account for changes in the measurement protocols or instrumentation over time, ensuring time series consistency. Homogenization algorithms identify breakpoints or shifts in the data and adjust them to create a homogeneous dataset.

Data Analysis:
Quantitative analysis of climate data involves applying statistical techniques to uncover trends, patterns, and relationships. Descriptive statistics, such as means, standard deviations, percentiles, and frequency distributions, provide a summary of the data distribution, central tendency, and variability. These measures help understand the characteristics of climate variables and provide a basis for comparison.

Time series analysis helps identify long-term trends, cyclic or oscillatory patterns, shifts in climate regimes, and seasonality in climate variables. Trend analysis techniques, such as linear regression, Mann-Kendall test, or Sen's slope estimator, assess the direction and magnitude of changes over time. Time series decomposition methods, such as seasonal decomposition of time series or empirical mode decomposition, separate the time series into different components, such as trend, seasonality, and noise, enabling a deeper understanding of the underlying patterns.

Spatial analysis techniques, including spatial autocorrelation, kriging, and geostatistics, allow for the examination of spatial patterns and heterogeneity across different regions. Spatial autocorrelation quantifies the degree of spatial dependence in the data, helping identify clusters or hotspots. Kriging, a geostatistical interpolation technique, estimates values at unobserved locations by incorporating spatial correlation information. Geostatistical analysis combines the spatial patterns observed at different locations to generate spatial predictions and uncertainty estimates.

Statistical tests, such as correlation analysis, regression models, and multivariate analysis, are used to investigate relationships between climate variables and other factors, such as anthropogenic activities, land-use change, or natural phenomena. Correlation analysis measures the strength and direction of association between variables. Regression models help assess the impact of different predictor variables on the climate response. Multivariate analysis, such as principal component analysis or factor analysis, reduces the complexity of the data and identifies underlying patterns or dominant modes of variability.

Furthermore, advanced techniques such as cluster analysis, machine learning algorithms, and neural networks can help identify distinct climate patterns, classify regions based on similarities or differences, and perform data-driven modeling and prediction. Cluster analysis groups similar locations or time periods based on their climate characteristics, aiding in regional climate classification or identification of climate zones. Machine learning algorithms, such as decision trees, random forests, or support vector machines, can identify complex relationships and patterns in the data without relying on predefined equations. Neural networks, inspired by the structure of the brain, can learn relationships and make predictions based on large amounts of data.

Interpretation:

The interpretation of quantitative climate data is crucial for making informed decisions and developing appropriate adaptation and mitigation strategies. The findings from the data analysis can help identify vulnerable regions, hotspot areas, and areas of concern. Analysis of extreme climatic events, such as heatwaves, droughts, heavy rainfall, and hurricanes, can provide insights into changing risk patterns and inform resilience-building measures. By understanding the spatial and temporal characteristics of climate change, policymakers, researchers, and stakeholders can prioritize interventions and allocate resources effectively. Furthermore, the interpretation should consider the uncertainty associated with the data and the limitations of the analysis techniques employed, ensuring that the findings are communicated accurately and transparently.

Conclusion:

Quantitative analysis of climate data provides crucial insights into the changing climate patterns and their potential impacts. Through systematic data collection, processing, and analysis, decision-makers can make informed choices and develop strategies to address the challenges posed by climate change. It is imperative to continue refining and updating these analyses as new data becomes available and as our understanding of climate change evolves. Integration of climate data analysis with socioeconomic data can facilitate comprehensive assessments of vulnerability, impacts, and adaptation options. By leveraging advanced analytical techniques and interdisciplinary collaborations, we can work towards a more sustainable and resilient future for our planet and its inhabitants.

Qualitative Analysis of Socio-Political Impacts

I n this chapter, we will delve into a qualitative analysis of the socio-political impacts of climate change in Arab regions. While previous chapters have focused on the scientific and economic aspects of climate change, it is crucial to examine the intricate relationship between climate change and its effects on society and politics. This analysis will provide a comprehensive understanding of the challenges and opportunities that arise in the face of climate change and guide policy responses for a sustainable future.

Methodology:
To conduct a qualitative analysis, we employed a combination of in-depth interviews, focus groups, and document analysis. These methods allowed us to capture the diverse perspectives and experiences of individuals and communities affected by climate change. Through these qualitative re-

search techniques, we aimed to uncover the underlying social and political dynamics at play in the wake of climate change impacts.

Key Findings:

1. Displacement and Migration:
Climate change-induced environmental changes, such as rising sea levels, extreme weather events, and droughts, have resulted in the displacement and migration of communities in Arab regions. Qualitative data revealed that entire villages have been uprooted, forcing people to relocate to safer areas. The interviews and focus groups provided evidence of the immense challenges faced by displaced individuals and families, including the loss of homes, livelihoods, and social connections. The emotional toll of displacement was also evident, with participants expressing a sense of loss, disruption, and uncertainty for their future. These findings highlight the urgent need for comprehensive support systems to address the immediate and long-term needs of displaced communities.

In-depth interviews conducted within affected communities shed light on the complexities and nuances of displacement and migration patterns triggered by climate change. They revealed that the decision to relocate is often not a simple and voluntary choice but a response to the compounding effects of recurring climate-related events. Communities faced with repeated floods, storms, or droughts suffer not only physical but also emotional and psychological damages. The lingering trauma may reshape their perception of their homeland, leading to a broader recognition that relocation is no longer a temporary measure, but a permanent solution to ensure safety and security for their families.

Further analysis of the interview data pointed out the unequal distribution of resources and vulnerabilities in both the areas of origin and the areas of relocation. The displacement process often exacerbates pre-existing social inequalities, creating new challenges for displaced individuals and communities, especially on the outskirts of urban areas where access to essential services and infrastructure is limited. These findings emphasise the need to go beyond addressing the immediate physical consequences of displacement and ensure comprehensive policies that address social disparities, empower marginalised groups, and provide adequate support for socio-economic integration in new locations.

2. Social Inequalities:

Qualitative analysis highlighted that climate change exacerbates existing social inequalities within Arab regions. Vulnerable groups, such as women, children, the elderly, and impoverished communities, bear the brunt of climate change impacts disproportionately. Interviews and focus group discussions revealed that women, in particular, face specific challenges as they are often responsible for securing water and food for their households, but increased resource scarcity makes this task even more difficult. Furthermore, marginalised groups, including those living in informal settlements or rural areas with limited access to basic services, are more susceptible to the adverse effects of climate change. The qualitative data emphasised the urgent need for policies that address social justice issues, such as gender equality and poverty reduction, in the face of climate change.

In-depth interviews and focus group discussions revealed that women, although disproportionately affected by climate change, also play critical roles as agents of change and resilience within their communities. Women have developed innovative strategies for coping with the impacts of climate change, such as promoting sustainable agricultural practises, engaging in income-generating activities, and advocating for gender-responsive policies. However, these efforts are often impeded by societal norms, limited access to resources, and unequal power dynamics. To address these challenges, it is crucial to amplify the voices and agency of women in decision-making processes, invest in their education and skills development, and provide them with equal access to economic opportunities and resources. Integrating a gender-responsive approach in policy frameworks will not only enhance the adaptive capacity of communities but also contribute to overall social equality and empowerment.

3. Conflict and Instability:

Qualitative research revealed the potential for increased conflict and political instability resulting from climate change impacts. Scarce resources, displacement, and growing social inequalities can create fertile ground for tension and unrest. The qualitative analysis shed light on how climate change can act as a catalyst for existing conflicts and contribute to new ones, threatening regional stability. Participants in the interviews and focus groups expressed concerns over water scarcity leading to disputes over shared water resources, with potential ramifications for diplomatic relationships between countries. The findings underscore the importance of building adaptive capacity, fostering cooperation, and resolving conflicts to maintain stability in the face of climate change challenges.

In-depth interviews conducted with experts in the field of political science and international relations revealed the intricate linkages between climate change and security in the Arab regions. They emphasised that the socio-political impacts of climate change have the potential to amplify existing conflicts, pose threats to human security, and destabilise regional dynamics. The documented cases of tensions arising from disputes over water resources, migration pressures, and competition for arable land serve as warning signs of potential future conflict escalation.

Furthermore, focus group discussions provided insights into the role of diplomacy and regional cooperation in managing climate change impacts. Participants stressed the importance of enhancing communication channels, sharing scientific research, and establishing frameworks for joint adaptation and mitigation efforts. They highlighted the need for multilateral agreements, political will, and strengthened cross-border collaborations to address shared climate change challenges effectively.

4. Adaptation and Resilience:
The qualitative data demonstrated that communities in Arab regions display remarkable resilience and adaptability in the face of climate change. Local knowledge, traditional practises, and community networks are vital resources that enable communities to cope with the challenges posed by climate change. Participants shared inspiring storeys of community-led initiatives, such as water management systems, agroforestry practises, and knowledge-sharing platforms, that promote adaptation and resilience. These initiatives not only address the socio-economic impacts of climate change but also foster a sense of ownership, empowerment, and social cohesion within the communities. The qualitative analysis highlighted the importance of recognising and supporting these grassroots efforts in policy frameworks.

In-depth interviews and focus group discussions provided in-depth insights into the adaptive strategies employed by communities in response to climate change impacts. Participants shared experiences of local knowledge systems, which often incorporate agroecological practises and traditional water management techniques. These practises, deeply rooted in cultural heritage, contribute significantly to sustainable resource use, water conservation, and land preservation. Moreover, community networks and social capital play a crucial role in sharing information, fostering collective action, and building solidarity in times of crisis.

The qualitative analysis further underscored the importance of integrating these local practises into wider policy frameworks. Recognising the value of indigenous knowledge, enhancing community participation in decision-making processes, and providing financial and technical support for community-led adaptation initiatives can contribute to more effective and locally appropriate solutions. Moreover, partnerships between local communities, NGOs, and government agencies can facilitate the exchange of knowledge, resources, and expertise to enhance community resilience and strengthen the overall societal response to climate change impacts.

Policy Implications:
Based on the qualitative analysis, it is evident that effective policy responses to climate change must go beyond scientific and economic considerations. Social and political dynamics should be central to policy frameworks. Policy-makers should consider the following key implications:

1. Comprehensive support systems for displaced communities: Policies should address the immediate and long-term needs of displaced communities, including access to housing, healthcare, education, and livelihood opportunities. Support systems should also address the emotional and psychological toll of displacement by providing counselling and mental health services.

2. Addressing social inequalities: Policies need to prioritise social justice, gender equality, and poverty reduction in the face of climate change impacts. This includes promoting women's empowerment, ensuring equal access to resources and opportunities, and addressing the needs of marginalised groups.

3. Conflict prevention and resolution: Policymakers need to prioritise conflict prevention and resolution strategies, recognising the potential

for climate change impacts to exacerbate existing conflicts and contribute to instability. This includes promoting diplomacy, regional cooperation, and joint adaptation and mitigation efforts.

4. Supporting community-led adaptation: Policies should recognise and support grassroots initiatives that promote community-led adaptation and resilience. This includes integrating indigenous knowledge and traditional practises into wider policy frameworks, fostering community participation in decision-making processes, and providing support for community-led initiatives.

5. Investing in education and awareness: Policies should prioritise education and awareness programmes on climate change impacts, adaptation strategies, and sustainable practises. This includes investing in formal and informal education systems, promoting knowledge-sharing platforms, and raising public awareness on climate change and its socio-political implications.

6. Strengthening governance and accountability: Policies should prioritise good governance practises, transparency, and accountability in addressing climate change impacts. This includes ensuring that decision-making processes are inclusive, participatory, and responsive to the needs of affected communities.

Conclusion:
Qualitative analysis of the socio-political impacts of climate change in Arab regions provides important insights into the complex dynamics at play. The findings underscore the urgent need for comprehensive and holistic policy responses that address the immediate and long-term needs of affected communities, promote social justice and equality, prevent conflicts, support community-led adaptation, and strengthen governance and

accountability. By integrating these key implications into policy frameworks, policymakers can effectively navigate the socio-political challenges and opportunities presented by climate change, ensuring a sustainable and resilient future for Arab regions.

Case Study Analysis: The Mediterranean

The Mediterranean region, known for its picturesque landscapes and rich cultural heritage, is facing significant challenges due to climate change. This chapter presents a comprehensive analysis of the impacts and responses of Mediterranean countries to climate change. By examining specific case studies within the Mediterranean, we aim to understand the unique vulnerabilities, strategies, and adaptation efforts implemented by these nations.

1. The Climate Change Context in the Mediterranean:
The Mediterranean region is known for its mild and dry summers, making it a popular destination for tourists from around the world. However, climate change poses significant threats to this region, with the Mediterranean experiencing more rapid warming than the global average. Rising sea levels, increasing temperatures, prolonged droughts, and more frequent extreme weather events are becoming increasingly common. These changes have profound implications for the region's ecosystems, agriculture, tourism, human health, and coastal infrastructure.

2. Case Study 1: Spain and its Coastal Vulnerabilities:

Spain, with its extensive coastline extending over 7,880 kilometres, offers a unique perspective on the vulnerability of Mediterranean countries to climate change. The country faces significant challenges such as coastal erosion, flooding, and impacts on its tourism industry. Coastal erosion has already resulted in the loss of valuable beachfront areas, threatening the structural integrity of coastal towns and cities. Public infrastructure, including roads, buildings, and utilities, is at risk. Additionally, extreme weather events, including storms and heavy rainfall, have led to increased flood risks along the coast. Spain has implemented innovative adaptation strategies such as the construction of artificial reefs, nourishment of beaches, and the restoration of dunes to mitigate these challenges and protect its coastline. These measures aim to maintain healthy and resilient coastal ecosystems while safeguarding the economic benefits derived from tourism activities.

3. Case Study 2: Greece and its Agricultural Adversities:

Greece, traditionally rooted in agriculture, grapples with the impacts of climate change on its agricultural practises. Changing precipitation patterns, increased wildfire risks, and water scarcity pose significant challenges to the farming sector. Greek farmers face difficulties in maintaining crop yields, preserving the quality of agricultural land, and sustaining rural livelihoods. The region's renowned olive groves, vineyards, and citrus orchards are particularly vulnerable. To address these adversities, Greece has adopted adaptive measures such as the promotion of climate-resilient crops, precision agriculture techniques, and improved water management practises. Agroforestry systems have also been implemented to enhance soil resilience and diversify income sources for farmers. Additionally, increased cooperation between farmers, local communities, and research institutions has played a crucial role in knowledge sharing and effective adaptation strategies.

4. Case Study 3: Italy and the Threat to Cultural Heritage:
Italy, a country steeped in history and home to numerous UNESCO World Heritage Sites, faces the risk of significant damage and loss due to climate change impacts. Rising sea levels, extreme weather events, and erosion pose direct threats to Italy's cultural heritage. Iconic sites such as Venice, Pompeii, and the Amalfi Coast are particularly vulnerable. Increased flooding in Venice, due to subsidence and rising sea levels, is leading to accelerated deterioration of the city's architectural treasures. Moreover, the shifting climate patterns are affecting the preservation of historic buildings, frescoes, and archaeological sites across the country. Italy has undertaken comprehensive actions to preserve and adapt its cultural heritage, including the construction of flood barriers in Venice, the implementation of conservation measures, and the development of climate change impact assessments for prioritising preservation efforts. These initiatives highlight the importance of integrating scientific knowledge with cultural heritage management to safeguard Italy's treasures for future generations.

5. Case Study 4: Turkey and Urban Resilience:
Turkey, with its rapidly growing urban centres, confronts unique challenges in the face of climate change. The country experiences extreme heatwaves, flooding, and changes in precipitation patterns, all of which impact Turkish cities and their populations. Urban areas face risks such as heat-related illnesses, water scarcity, and increased vulnerability to natural disasters. Istanbul, the country's largest city, is particularly susceptible to coastal flooding due to sea-level rise. To address these challenges, Turkey has prioritised urban planning and infrastructure resilience to enhance adaptability. Measures include the development of heatwave action plans, the construction of green spaces and cooling corridors, and the incorpora-

tion of climate change considerations into city planning regulations. These efforts aim to create sustainable, livable cities that can withstand climate change impacts while ensuring the wellbeing of their inhabitants.

6. Lessons Learnt and Best Practises:
Drawing from the case studies in the Mediterranean region, several key lessons and best practises emerge. Firstly, it is evident that climate change adaptation and resilience require interdisciplinary collaboration, with active participation from academia, government institutions, civil society, and local communities. Robust data collection and analysis facilitate evidence-based decision-making and help implement context-specific solutions. Community engagement and knowledge-sharing platforms, such as farmer networks or heritage preservation associations, are crucial in developing and implementing effective adaptation strategies. Furthermore, policy integration across various sectors, including agriculture, tourism, and urban planning, is essential for holistic adaptation frameworks and strategies. These policies should also prioritise the integration of climate change considerations into national development plans and local bylaws to ensure long-term resilience.

7. Recommendations for Policy Frameworks:
Based on the analysis of the Mediterranean case studies, it is evident that a robust policy framework is crucial for addressing climate change challenges effectively. Policymakers must prioritise the integration of climate change considerations into decision-making processes across sectors at national, regional, and local levels. This involves establishing early warning systems, strengthening climate change education and awareness programmes, and promoting sustainable practises such as transitioning to renewable energy sources, improving water management, and supporting nature-based solutions. Furthermore, forging stronger international collaborations and partnerships within the Mediterranean region can facili-

tate knowledge exchange, funding opportunities, and joint efforts to combat climate change effectively. Initiatives such as joint research projects, sharing of best practises, and capacity-building programmes can enhance the resilience of Mediterranean countries collectively.

8. Conclusion:

In conclusion, the Mediterranean region faces significant climate change challenges that demand immediate action. Through a combination of innovative strategies, policy integration, community engagement, and international cooperation, Mediterranean countries can build resilience and ensure a sustainable future for their populations, ecosystems, cultural heritage, and economies. The case studies presented in this chapter highlight the urgency of addressing climate change impacts, as well as the potential for tailored and context-specific solutions. By learning from each other's experiences and integrating scientific knowledge with local expertise, Mediterranean countries can pave the way towards a more resilient and climate-resilient future.

Impacts and Responses in the Mediterranean

The Mediterranean region, renowned for its diverse cultures, fascinating history, and picturesque landscapes, is confronting an escalating array of challenges as a result of the impacts of climate change. Scientists and researchers have observed a discernible shift in temperature patterns, alterations in precipitation levels, and rising sea levels, all of which have engendered significant threats to the region's ecosystems, economies, and societies. In order to adequately address these challenges, comprehensive and integrated approaches are imperative, taking into account the unique characteristics and vulnerabilities that define the Mediterranean region.

One of the paramount impacts of climate change in the Mediterranean region is the amplified occurrence of extreme weather events. Heatwaves of unprecedented intensity, prolonged droughts, and intense rainfall events have become more frequent, undermining traditional agricultural practises and exacerbating water scarcity issues. Agriculture holds immense importance in the Mediterranean, with many countries relying heavily on this sector for food security and livelihoods. However, as temperatures rise and rainfall becomes erratic, farmers and agricultural communities are grappling with declining crop yields and heightened vulnerability to food insecurity. The adverse effects of decreasing agricultural productivity extend beyond economic setbacks, impacting social cohesion and exacerbating inequality, as rural communities face displacement and dwindling opportunities.

Moreover, the Mediterranean region's extensive coastline, boasting a multitude of vibrant cities, popular tourist destinations, and critical infrastructure, faces numerous challenges due to climate change. Rising sea levels, increased erosion rates, and more frequent and intense storms threaten coastal communities with unprecedented force. Many cities and towns along the coast are experiencing shoreline retreat, resulting in the loss of valuable land and infrastructure. The tourism sector, a vital source of revenue and employment for Mediterranean countries, is particularly susceptible to climate change impacts. The erosion of beaches, degradation of marine ecosystems, and the heightened frequency of extreme weather events collectively jeopardise the sustainability of the tourism industry, amplifying the socio-economic consequences of climate change, including unemployment, business closures, and regional disparities.

In response to these pressing challenges, Mediterranean countries have initiated a range of adaptation measures, prioritising the protection of vulnerable populations and ecosystems. An integrated approach to water management stands as a crucial facet in adaptation efforts. Governments are constructing reservoirs, promoting water-saving technologies, and advocating for efficient irrigation practises to ensure adequate water availability for both agricultural and domestic use, reducing reliance on limited water resources. Furthermore, countries are investing in research and development to enhance their understanding of hydrological systems, improve water monitoring capabilities, and foster effective water governance structures for sustainable water management.

Sustainable coastal management represents another pivotal focus in the Mediterranean's adaptation initiatives. Governments are implementing measures to safeguard coastlines, restore degraded ecosystems such as dunes, wetlands, and coral reefs, and enhance resilience to sea-level rise. These efforts entail collaborative approaches involving various stakeholders, including local communities, scientists, and policymakers, to develop comprehensive plans incorporating ecological, social, and economic considerations. Embracing innovative approaches, such as nature-based solutions, including the restoration of coastal wetlands and the creation of artificial reefs, can deliver multifaceted benefits, such as habitat restoration, coastal protection, and carbon sequestration.

Furthermore, the Mediterranean region recognises the importance of adopting an international and regional approach to addressing climate change impacts. Enhanced cooperation and knowledge-sharing among countries transcend borders, acknowledging the transboundary nature of climate change impacts. Regional initiatives like the Union for the Mediterranean and the Mediterranean Strategy for Sustainable Development serve as vital platforms for dialogue, policy coordination, and collaborative project implementation. These initiatives foster the sharing of best practises, exchange of information, and mobilisation of financial resources to support adaptation and mitigation measures across the region.

While adaptation measures are crucial, Mediterranean countries also acknowledge the significance of mitigating climate change. As such, they have been implementing policies and projects to promote cleaner and more sustainable energy systems. The development of renewable energy sources such as solar and wind power is gaining momentum, with countries undertaking large-scale projects and prioritising energy efficiency measures. Additionally, the transition to low-carbon transportation systems, including the promotion of electric vehicles and the improvement of public transportation infrastructure, is being pursued to decrease emissions from the transport sector.

To conclude, the Mediterranean region finds itself grappling with the mounting impacts of climate change, necessitating immediate and concerted action. The preservation of its unique environment, protection of coastal communities, and the establishment of socio-economic stability pose formidable challenges. Through a combination of comprehensive adaptation and mitigation measures, coupled with regional cooperation and international support, the countries bordering the Mediterranean can effectively address these challenges and construct a more resilient and sustainable future. However, time is of the essence, and transformative efforts must be undertaken promptly to ensure the preservation of a prosperous and sustainable Mediterranean in the face of an ever-changing climate.

CASE STUDY ANALYSIS: THE GULF

In this chapter, we will delve into a comprehensive case study analysis of the Gulf region, exploring the impacts of climate change and the responses implemented to address these challenges. The Gulf region, comprising countries such as Saudi Arabia, United Arab Emirates, Qatar, Kuwait, Bahrain, and Oman, faces unique environmental vulnerabilities due to its geographical location and reliance on natural resources. By examining the vulnerabilities of the region and the specific impacts of climate change, as well as the responses and initiatives implemented by these nations, we can gain valuable insights into the complex interplay between climate change and socio-economic dynamics in the Gulf.

1. Vulnerabilities of the Gulf Region:

The Gulf region is characterised by its arid climate, limited freshwater sources, and extensive coastline. The geographical location of the region exposes it to the impacts of climate change, making it highly susceptible to various environmental vulnerabilities. These include:

a) Rising sea levels: With a substantial portion of the Gulf region located along its coastlines, rising sea levels pose a significant threat. Coastal erosion, flooding, and saltwater intrusion into freshwater aquifers are potential consequences that can disrupt vital economic sectors such as tourism, fisheries, and agriculture. The Gulf Cooperation Council's (GCC) coastal areas are expected to experience an average sea-level rise of 18-30 cm by 2050, increasing the vulnerability of coastal communities and infrastructure.

b) Water scarcity: The Gulf region faces water scarcity due to its arid climate and limited freshwater resources. The demand for water, both for domestic consumption and industrial needs, is increasing rapidly. Climate change exacerbates water scarcity by raising temperatures, increasing evaporation rates, and reducing water availability. This puts additional pressure on the region's already strained water resources, demanding innovative water management strategies. The per capita water availability in the GCC countries is significantly lower than the global average, and it is projected to further decline in the coming years.

c) Extreme heatwaves: The Gulf region already experiences scorching temperatures, with some areas recording some of the highest temperatures in the world. Climate change intensifies heatwaves, which can have severe health impacts, especially for vulnerable populations. Heatwaves also affect productivity, energy consumption, and overall quality of life. The frequency and intensity of heatwaves are projected to increase, with temperatures in the Gulf region expected to exceed the threshold for human comfort and adaptation.

d) Marine ecosystem degradation: The Gulf region boasts diverse and unique marine ecosystems, including coral reefs and mangroves. However, rising temperatures and ocean acidification due to climate change threaten these fragile ecosystems. Coral bleaching, loss of biodiversity, and disruption of fisheries can have far-reaching ecological, economic, and social consequences. The Red Sea and the Arabian Gulf are known for their rich marine biodiversity, but the rising temperatures and increasing acidity of the waters jeopardise the survival of many species, ultimately impacting the region's natural heritage and fishing industry.

2. Impacts of Climate Change in the Gulf:

a) Sea-level rise: The Gulf region's low-lying coastal areas are highly susceptible to the consequences of sea-level rise. Coastal erosion, loss of coastal habitats, and increased vulnerability to storm surge and extreme weather events are among the impacts observed. The degradation of coastal ecosystems also poses a risk to important infrastructure, including ports, airports, and coastal cities. Urgent action is needed to protect vulnerable coastal areas, through the construction of seawalls, restoration of habitats like mangroves, and the implementation of integrated coastal zone management plans.

b) Water scarcity: The arid nature of the Gulf region, coupled with climate change impacts, intensifies the water scarcity challenge. Groundwater resources, often used for drinking water and agriculture, are at risk of salinisation due to rising sea levels. Decreased rainfall and increased evaporation rates further exacerbate water scarcity. This poses significant challenges to the sustainability of agricultural practises, requires increased reliance on energy-intensive desalination processes, and impacts overall water availability for domestic and industrial users. Integrated water resource management and the promotion of water-saving technologies are crucial for sustainable water management in the region.

c) Extreme heatwaves: The Gulf region already experiences extreme heatwaves, and climate change exacerbates this reality. Heat stress poses severe health risks, including heatstroke and dehydration. Outdoor workers, disadvantaged communities, and the elderly are particularly vulnerable. The increased cooling demands in buildings heighten energy consumption, further straining resources and contributing to greenhouse gas emissions. Adaptation measures such as urban heat island mitigation strategies, improved building design, and public awareness campaigns can help reduce the health impacts of extreme heat.

d) Marine ecosystem degradation: The unique marine ecosystems of the Gulf region are under threat due to climate change. Rising sea temperatures and ocean acidification impact the health and biodiversity of coral reefs, damaging their ability to provide habitat, protect coastlines, and support fisheries. Mangroves, critical coastal ecosystems protecting against erosion and providing valuable breeding grounds for marine life, are also at risk of degradation. The loss of these ecosystems affects the region's natural heritage, biodiversity, and economic activities like fishing and tourism. Conservation efforts, including the establishment of marine protected areas, restoration projects, and sustainable fishing practises, are vital for the preservation and resilience of these ecosystems.

3. Climate Change Responses:

a) Diversification of the economy: Recognising the risks climate change poses to traditional sectors such as oil and gas, Gulf countries have initiated efforts to diversify their economies. By investing in renewable energy projects, such as solar and wind power, and promoting the development of green technologies, these nations aim to reduce their carbon footprint and reliance on fossil fuels. The promotion of sustainable tourism and eco-friendly practises also contribute to economic diversification. The

UAE's Masdar City project, which aims to be a sustainable city with zero-carbon emissions, is a prime example of the region's commitment to economic diversification and clean energy transitions.

b) Water management strategies: Gulf countries focus on strategic water management as a response to water scarcity. Desalination plants, capable of converting seawater into freshwater, play a crucial role in meeting the region's water demands. Additionally, various initiatives are in place to encourage water conservation, wastewater reuse, and rainwater harvesting. Governments further emphasise efficient irrigation techniques, crop selection suited to the arid climate, and integrated water resource management. Recycling and treating wastewater for agricultural purposes can significantly reduce the pressure on freshwater resources.

c) Building resilient infrastructure: Gulf countries invest in building resilient infrastructure capable of withstanding the impacts of climate change. This includes designing buildings and urban spaces with improved insulation to minimise energy consumption, utilising solar energy for cooling systems, and implementing policies for green building design and construction. Furthermore, the construction of seawalls and flood protection measures enhances resilience against coastal risks like storm surges and sea-level rise. The UAE's "Estidama" programme and Qatar's "Tarsheed" initiative are examples of sustainable building and energy efficiency programmes implemented in the region.

d) International cooperation: The Gulf region actively engages in international collaborations to address climate change challenges more effectively. Participating in global climate agreements, such as the Paris Agreement, enables these nations to contribute to global efforts to reduce greenhouse gas emissions. Additionally, sharing best practises, knowledge, and technology transfers with international partners fosters regional and global cooperation to address common climate change challenges. The UAE's hosting of the Abu Dhabi Sustainability Week and the DubaiSustainability Week are examples of platforms where international stakeholders come together to exchange ideas, showcase innovative solutions, and collaborate on climate change mitigation and adaptation.

e) Research and innovation: Gulf countries invest in research and innovation to better understand the impacts of climate change and develop sustainable solutions. Research institutions, such as the Masdar Institute in the UAE and the Qatar Environment and Energy Research Institute, focus on renewable energy, environmental conservation, and sustainable development. These institutions collaborate with international partners to develop technologies and strategies for climate change adaptation and mitigation, including the development of advanced desalination techniques, renewable energy technologies, and climate modelling.

f) Public awareness and education: Gulf countries emphasise public awareness and education to mobilise their societies and create a sense of responsibility towards climate change. Campaigns and initiatives are in place to educate communities about the impacts of climate change, promote sustainable lifestyles, and encourage behaviour change. Education programmes at schools and universities integrate climate change and environmental sustainability into their curricula, fostering a culture of environmental stewardship and sustainability.

Conclusion:

The case study analysis of the Gulf region underscores the unique vulnerabilities of this region to climate change impacts. Rising sea levels, water scarcity, extreme heatwaves, and marine ecosystem degradation are among the key challenges faced by Gulf countries. However, these nations have responded proactively by implementing a range of initiatives and strategies to adapt to and mitigate the impacts of climate change. Economic diversification, water management strategies, resilient infrastructure, international cooperation, research and innovation, and public awareness and education are some of the key responses undertaken by Gulf countries.

While progress has been made, the Gulf region still faces significant challenges in addressing climate change effectively. Continued efforts are needed to further invest in renewable energy, improve water management practises, enhance resilience of infrastructure and coastal areas, and advance research and innovation in climate change solutions. By adopting a holistic and integrated approach, the Gulf countries can navigate the complex interplay between climate change and socio-economic dynamics, ensuring a sustainable and resilient future for the region.

IMPACTS AND RESPONSES IN THE Gulf

T he Gulf region, with its strategic location and vast oil reserves, has experienced significant economic growth over the past few decades. However, this region is not immune to the impacts of climate change. Rising sea levels, extreme heatwaves, water scarcity, and ecosystem degradation are some of the challenges that Gulf countries are facing. This chapter delves deeper into the impacts of climate change in the Gulf and explores the responses that have been implemented to mitigate its effects.

Impacts of Climate Change in the Gulf:

1. Rising sea levels: The Gulf coastline is highly vulnerable to rising sea levels due to its low elevation and sandy soils. The combination of sea-level rise and storm surges poses a significant threat to coastal cities, tourist infrastructure, and oil and gas installations. Coastal erosion and increased flooding not only damage the environment but also have substantial eco-

nomic implications.

2. Extreme heatwaves: The Gulf region already experiences scorching temperatures during summer months, but climate change exacerbates this issue. Heatwaves are becoming longer and more intense, surpassing historical records. Extreme heat poses a severe health risk, leading to heat exhaustion, heatstroke, and even death, particularly among vulnerable populations. Outdoor workers, infants, the elderly, and individuals with pre-existing health conditions are especially susceptible to these extreme temperatures.

3. Water scarcity: The Gulf has limited freshwater resources, relying mainly on desalination and groundwater extraction. However, climate change is intensifying water scarcity challenges. Rising temperatures accelerate evaporation rates, reducing the availability of freshwater for domestic, agricultural, and industrial purposes. This situation becomes more challenging as water demand continues to increase due to population growth, economic development, and urbanisation.

4. Ecosystem degradation: Climate change is negatively impacting the fragile ecosystems of the Gulf, including coral reefs, mangroves, and marine habitats. Rising sea temperatures, ocean acidification, and pollution pose threats to the biodiversity and productivity of the region's marine life. Coral bleaching events, caused by increased water temperatures, can lead to the collapse of coral reef ecosystems, affecting vital fishery resources, coastal protection against storm surges, and ecosystem services such as water filtration.

Responses to Climate Change in the Gulf:

1. Renewable energy investments: Gulf countries recognise the impor-

tance of diversifying their energy sources and reducing their dependence on fossil fuels. Significant investments have been made in renewable energy projects, particularly solar and wind energy. For instance, Saudi Arabia's Vision 2030 aims to develop 58.7 gigawatts (GW) of renewable energy by 2030. Abu Dhabi's Masdar City, a sustainable urban development, is powered by renewable energy sources and aims to be carbon-neutral. These initiatives promote the growth of a clean energy sector, reduce greenhouse gas emissions, and enhance energy security.

2. Water conservation measures: Recognising the importance of water security, Gulf countries have implemented various measures to conserve and manage water resources effectively. Advanced desalination technologies have been developed to improve the efficiency of freshwater production. Additionally, wastewater treatment and reuse systems are being implemented to maximise water availability. Public awareness campaigns and policies promoting responsible water usage, efficient irrigation methods, and sustainable agricultural practises are also integral to water conservation efforts.

3. Sustainable urban planning: Gulf cities are embracing sustainable urban planning to mitigate the impacts of climate change on their populations and environments. Green infrastructure, such as vertical gardens, rooftop gardens, and urban forests, is being incorporated to improve air quality, reduce the urban heat island effect, and enhance biodiversity. Energy-efficient buildings, smart grid systems, and integrated public transportation networks are also being integrated into urban planning to reduce carbon emissions and enhance urban resilience.

4. International collaborations and agreements: Gulf countries actively participate in international agreements and collaborations to address the global challenges of climate change. The Gulf Cooperation Council

(GCC) fosters regional cooperation on various environmental projects, including clean energy development, environmental conservation, and climate change research. Gulf nations also engage with global forums, such as the United Nations Climate Change Conferences, to share their experiences, learn from best practises, and contribute to the global dialogue on climate action.

Conclusion:

The Gulf region faces significant challenges due to climate change, but proactive responses are being implemented to mitigate its impacts. Through renewable energy investments, water conservation measures, sustainable urban planning, and international collaborations, Gulf countries are working towards a more sustainable and resilient future. However, continuous efforts and collaborative actions are needed to effectively address the complex and interconnected issues posed by climate change in the Gulf. By adopting innovative technologies, fostering sustainable practises, and engaging in global partnerships, the Gulf region can thrive in the face of climate change while preserving its natural heritage and promoting the well-being of its inhabitants. The journey towards sustainability requires a long-term vision, consistent commitment, and active engagement from all stakeholders to build a prosperous and resilient Gulf region that can adapt and thrive in a changing climate.

CASE STUDY ANALYSIS: THE INDIAN OCEAN

The Indian Ocean represents one of the most diverse and ecologically rich regions on our planet. Its unique geographical location and climatic patterns make it a critical area to investigate the impacts of climate change. In this chapter, we will delve into a detailed case study analysis of the Indian Ocean, examining the specific challenges it faces and the responses that have been implemented to address the growing threats.

Background on the Indian Ocean:
The Indian Ocean, with an area of approximately 73.5 million square kilometres, encompasses a wide range of ecosystems, including coral reefs, mangroves, seagrass meadows, and open ocean habitats. This vast area provides habitat for various marine species, some of which are found nowhere else on Earth. The region is also a vital corridor for global trade, facilitating the movement of goods and connecting nations from East Africa to the Arabian Peninsula, the Indian subcontinent, and Southeast Asia.

The Indian Ocean region is home to a multitude of nations, each with its own socio-economic and cultural characteristics. From the Maldives to Somalia, coastal regions surrounding the Indian Ocean have long relied on the ocean's resources for their livelihoods, including fishing, tourism, and trade. The diverse communities in this region depend on the health and resilience of the ocean ecosystems for their economic well-being and survival.

Impacts of Climate Change:
The effects of climate change are already being felt in the Indian Ocean region, with significant consequences on both the environment and human populations. Rising sea levels, primarily caused by the melting of polar ice caps and the expansion of warm seawater, pose a major threat to vulnerable coastal areas. Small island nations, such as the Maldives and Seychelles, are particularly at risk, as their low-lying lands are highly susceptible to inundation and increased coastal erosion.

In addition to sea-level rise, the Indian Ocean region has witnessed an increase in cyclonic activities. More frequent and intense tropical storms, fuelled by warmer sea surface temperatures, not only cause devastating damage to coastal infrastructure, ecosystems, and human lives, but also lead to long-term socio-economic setbacks for affected communities. The aftermath of these storms often involves significant challenges in recovery and rebuilding, further exacerbating the vulnerabilities of coastal regions.

Another concerning impact of climate change in the Indian Ocean is the degradation of coral reefs. The rising sea temperatures and ocean acidification, resulting from increased carbon dioxide levels, contribute to coral bleaching, a process in which corals expel the symbiotic algae that give them their vibrant colours and provide vital nutrients. Coral bleaching weakens the coral structures, making them more susceptible to disease and eventual death. Coral reefs are crucial ecosystems, providing habitat for

thousands of species, protecting coastlines from wave damage, and supporting tourism and local economies. The loss of these vibrant ecosystems
poses a significant threat to both marine biodiversity and the livelihoods
of coastal communities.

Responses and Adaptation Strategies:
Governments and local communities within the Indian Ocean region
have recognised the urgent need to adapt to these changing conditions and
implement mitigation strategies. Various adaptation strategies have been
implemented, focusing on both short-term and long-term measures to
build resilience and ensure sustainability.

One key strategy is coastal protection measures, such as constructing sea
walls, embankments, and artificial reefs. These measures aim to safeguard
vulnerable areas from erosion and inundation caused by rising sea levels
and storm surges. In addition to physical structures, nature-based solutions, such as restoring mangroves and seagrass meadows, are being implemented. These natural buffers can absorb wave energy, reduce erosion,
and provide habitat for a variety of marine species. They also act as carbon
sinks, helping mitigate climate change impacts.

Promoting sustainable fishing practises is another crucial aspect of adaptation in the Indian Ocean region. Overfishing and destructive fishing methods can significantly deplete fish populations and harm marine ecosystems.
Through the implementation of catch limits, promoting selective fishing
techniques, and establishing marine protected areas (MPAs), governments
and communities aim to regulate fishing activities and allow fish stocks to
recover. MPAs provide a means to protect and preserve vulnerable ecosystems, allowing them to regenerate and build resilience to climate change
impacts.

International Collaboration and Partnerships:

Recognising the transboundary nature of the challenges faced in the Indian Ocean, regional cooperation and international partnerships have emerged as important mechanisms for addressing climate change impacts. Organisations such as the Indian Ocean Rim Association (IORA), the Intergovernmental Oceanographic Commission (IOC), and the United Nations Environment Programme (UNEP) have played significant roles in facilitating knowledge sharing, capacity building, and funding opportunities.

Through international collaboration, countries within the Indian Ocean region have been able to access financial resources and expertise to develop comprehensive strategies and action plans. These collaborations have also facilitated the exchange of data and scientific research to better understand the specific impacts of climate change in the region. Moreover, regional institutions have played a vital role in fostering dialogue and cooperation among nations, encouraging collective action, and shared responsibility.

Conclusion:

The extended case study analysis of the Indian Ocean provides a deep understanding of the urgent need for proactive measures to address the impacts of climate change in the region. The diverse communities residing along the Indian Ocean have recognised the interdependence of their environment and livelihoods and are working together to find innovative solutions that ensure the resilience and sustainability of their ecosystems and well-being.

By establishing and strengthening effective adaptation measures, engaging in international cooperation, and promoting sustainable practises, it is possible for the Indian Ocean region to mitigate the worst impacts of climate change and create a more resilient future. Policymakers, researchers, and communities must remain committed to finding innovative and sustainable solutions as they learn valuable lessons from the Indian Ocean case study. The knowledge gained from this case study can be applied to other vulnerable regions globally, fostering global collaboration to address climate change and create a more sustainable and resilient world.

IMPACTS AND RESPONSES IN THE INDIAN OCEAN

T he Indian Ocean region is a vast expanse of water, encompassing multiple countries and ecosystems. As climate change continues to accelerate, this region is experiencing a range of profound impacts. From rising sea levels and increased frequency of extreme weather events to disruptions in marine biodiversity and threats to coastal communities, the consequences of climate change in the Indian Ocean are far-reaching. In this chapter, we will explore these impacts in detail and examine the various responses taken by governments, communities, and international organisations to mitigate and adapt to the challenges posed by climate change.

Impacts on Coastal Communities:

Coastal communities in the Indian Ocean are particularly vulnerable to the effects of climate change. Rising sea levels threaten the very existence of low-lying islands and coastal areas, leading to increased erosion, inundation, and salinisation of freshwater sources. Small island nations, such as the Maldives and Seychelles, are on the front lines of this crisis, as they face the potential loss of their entire territories. The displacement of communities and the loss of ancestral lands due to sea-level rise not only pose immediate challenges for housing, infrastructure, and livelihoods but also fuel social and political tensions.

In response to these challenges, coastal communities are adopting innovative adaptation strategies. For instance, the construction of sea walls and the use of innovative engineering techniques such as "building with nature" approaches are being employed to mitigate the impacts of rising sea levels and storm surges. These nature-based solutions include the restoration of natural coastal features like mangrove forests, coral reefs, and seagrass beds, which act as protective barriers against erosion and flooding while providing additional ecological benefits.

The increased frequency and intensity of cyclones and tropical storms are also taking a toll on coastal settlements in the Indian Ocean region. The devastating effects of these events result in loss of lives, destruction of infrastructure, and severe economic setbacks. Vulnerable communities are finding it increasingly difficult to recover and rebuild after each disaster, further exacerbating their vulnerability to future climatic events. However, efforts are being made to enhance disaster preparedness and response systems. Early warning systems, efficient evacuation plans, and community-based organisations are being strengthened to reduce the risk to lives and enhance resilience.

Impacts on Marine Biodiversity:
The Indian Ocean is known for its rich biodiversity, with its coral reefs, seagrass beds, and mangrove forests supporting a myriad of species. However, climate change is disrupting this delicate balance. Rising water tem-

peratures, resulting from greenhouse gas emissions, are causing widespread coral bleaching events. Coral reefs provide essential habitat for countless marine species, including economically important ones such as fish and shellfish. The loss of these habitats not only affects biodiversity but also threatens the livelihoods of fishing communities and the tourism industry, which heavily relies on the allure of diverse marine ecosystems.

To address the decline of coral reefs, conservation efforts are being scaled up in the Indian Ocean region. Coral nurseries are established to propagate coral fragments and restore degraded reef areas. Innovative techniques like micro-fragmentation are being employed to accelerate coral growth and aid in the recovery of damaged reefs. Additionally, artificial reef structures are being deployed to provide new habitat for marine life and promote ecosystem regeneration.

Ocean acidification is another consequence of climate change that directly impacts the Indian Ocean's marine biodiversity. As seawater absorbs more carbon dioxide from the atmosphere, its pH decreases, making it more acidic. This acidification process poses a significant threat to coral reefs, shellfish, and other organisms with calcium carbonate shells or skeletons. These changes disrupt the food web, as some species struggle to adapt or find alternate sources of sustenance. The cascading effects can have far-reaching consequences, not only on local fisheries and ecosystems but also on global food security and the balance of carbon uptake by marine systems.

To combat ocean acidification, research efforts are aimed at developing strategies to reduce carbon emissions and remove excess carbon dioxide from the atmosphere. Additionally, innovative marine technologies are being explored, such as the potential for offshore seaweed farming, as seaweed absorbs carbon dioxide and can help counteract ocean acidification.

Government and Community Responses:

Recognising the urgency of the situation, governments in the Indian Ocean region have begun implementing various strategies to address the impacts of climate change. Many countries have developed national climate change adaptation plans, which outline actions and policies to reduce vulnerability and enhance resilience. These plans commonly include measures such as the construction of coastal defences, the relocation of vulnerable communities, the promotion of renewable energy, and the adaptation of agriculture to changing conditions. Governments are also working toward improving early warning systems for storms and investing in infrastructure resilience to reduce the impact of extreme weather events.

At the regional level, the Indian Ocean Rim Association (IORA) has been promoting collaboration among member countries to address climate change impacts collectively. Through various working groups and initiatives, IORA facilitates knowledge sharing, capacity building, and the development of regional policies and strategies. The organisation encourages the exchange of best practises and provides technical assistance to member states in implementing climate change adaptation and mitigation measures.

Community-level responses are equally crucial in building resilience and adapting to the changing climate. Local communities are implementing innovative solutions, often with support from non-governmental organisations (NGOs) and international organisations. For example, the restoration of degraded coastal ecosystems, such as mangrove reforestation projects, can help mitigate the impacts of sea-level rise by providing natural buffers against storm surges and protecting against erosion. Similarly, the adoption of climate-smart agricultural practises, such as water-efficient irrigation and crop diversification, can enhance food security and resilience in the face of changing rainfall patterns.

Conclusion:

The impacts of climate change in the Indian Ocean region are undeniable and demand urgent action. The threats faced by coastal communities and marine biodiversity necessitate a comprehensive and collaborative approach. Governments, communities, NGOs, and international organisations must work together to develop adaptive strategies and mobilise resources to address the challenges posed by climate change. By implementing resilient infrastructure, promoting sustainable livelihoods, and protecting marine ecosystems, it is possible to mitigate the impacts and build resilience in the Indian Ocean region, ensuring a sustainable future for both its people and its diverse ecosystems. By nurturing the ecosystem and employing adaptive measures across multiple levels, we can create a foundation of resilience to weather the storms of climate change.

CROSS-REGIONAL COMPARISONS

In this chapter, we will delve even deeper into the cross-regional comparisons of the impacts and responses to climate change in different parts of the world. By examining multiple regions and their experiences, we can gain a more comprehensive understanding of the common challenges, unique dynamics, and potential solutions in each region.

One of the key findings from these cross-regional comparisons is the universality and urgency of the impacts of climate change. Climate change knows no boundaries and affects communities around the globe. However, the specific manifestations and severity of these impacts vary from one region to another, causing distinct vulnerabilities and requiring tailored responses.

In the Mediterranean region, for instance, increasing temperatures, prolonged droughts, and heightened risk of wildfires have become pressing issues. These challenges have significant implications for agriculture, water resources, and tourism, which are key sectors in the region. With higher temperatures and reduced rainfall, the availability of freshwater resources becomes a growing concern. In response, countries in the Mediterranean region have been implementing various adaptation strategies, such as water-efficient irrigation systems, desalination plants, and awareness campaigns to promote responsible water use. Additionally, efforts to diversify agricultural practises and promote sustainable tourism have gained traction, creating economic opportunities while reducing environmental impacts.

Conversely, in the Gulf region, rising sea levels and extreme heatwaves pose a direct threat to human health and infrastructure. With a substantial population living along the coast, there is an urgent need to protect vulnerable communities from coastal erosion and flooding. Adaptation measures in this region include building sea defences, enhancing urban planning, and implementing early warning systems for extreme weather events. The dependence on oil and gas revenues adds another layer of complexity to the region's response to climate change. Gulf countries are increasingly recognising the importance of economic diversification and sustainable development to ensure long-term resilience.

In the Indian Ocean, the impacts of climate change manifest in intensified cyclones, coastal erosion, and coral bleaching. Coastal communities and marine ecosystems are particularly vulnerable, impacting livelihoods and biodiversity. Coastal erosion not only displaces communities but also destroys critical infrastructure, such as ports and roads. To address these challenges, countries in the Indian Ocean region have been investing in coastal protection measures, mangrove restoration, and promoting community-based adaptation strategies. Additionally, efforts to reduce greenhouse gas emissions and promote renewable energy sources are gaining momentum.

Notably, these cross-regional comparisons also reveal that climate change responses must consider social and economic dimensions. While all regions face similar environmental challenges, the social and economic context in which these challenges arise significantly influences the available adaptive strategies and their effectiveness. For instance, in regions heavily reliant on specific industries such as agriculture or tourism, identifying alternative income streams and promoting sustainable practises is crucial for long-term resilience.

Despite these distinct regional variations, there are also commonalities in the responses to climate change. There is a growing recognition of the need for integrated and holistic approaches to adaptation and mitigation strategies. Cross-sectoral collaboration and coordination, involving government agencies, civil society organisations, and the private sector, are vital for effective response measures. This collaborative approach is evident in initiatives such as the Paris Agreement, where countries come together to pursue global climate goals.

Furthermore, the importance of international cooperation and sharing of knowledge and best practises cannot be overstated. The challenges faced by regions affected by climate change are interconnected, and solutions require global collective action. Collaborative initiatives such as technology transfers, capacity building, and financial support are essential for enabling adaptation and resilience. Global climate conferences, research partnerships, and platforms for knowledge exchange foster the sharing of experiences and expertise.

One striking aspect that emerges from these cross-regional comparisons is the critical role of governance and policy frameworks in addressing climate change effectively. Effective policies, supported by robust legal and institutional frameworks, have the potential to drive transformative change. Governments play a central role in creating an enabling environment that encourages sustainable practises, incentivises innovation, and fosters community participation. Regulatory measures, such as carbon pricing mechanisms and emissions reduction targets, can provide economic incentives for industries to shift toward low-carbon practises. Transparent and accountable governance structures ensure that climate action plans are implemented efficiently and fairly.

Another important consideration is the role of local communities in climate change adaptation. They possess valuable knowledge and adaptive capacities that can contribute to resilience-building efforts. Empowering communities through participatory decision-making processes and incorporating their traditional knowledge systems can lead to more tailored and sustainable solutions. Building community resilience involves providing access to climate information, offering technical support, and developing social safety nets to address the most vulnerable members.

As we delve further into cross-regional comparisons, it becomes evident that the challenges and opportunities associated with climate change are complex and interlinked. No single region or country can tackle these challenges in isolation. It requires concerted efforts and collaboration on a global scale. Enhancing international cooperation, supporting vulnerable regions, and accelerating the transition to a low-carbon economy are all crucial to effectively address climate change.

In the concluding chapter, we will summarise the key findings from our cross-regional comparisons and provide recommendations for policymakers and the general public. Our aim is to foster a sense of urgency and encourage collective action to address the impacts of climate change and build a sustainable future for all.

Lessons Learnt and Best Practices

Throughout this book, we have explored the impacts of climate change on small islands and peninsulas, specifically focusing on the regions of the Mediterranean, the Gulf, and the Indian Ocean. In this chapter, we will reflect on the lessons learnt from our research and highlight the best practises that have emerged in response to climate change challenges. By examining successful strategies and approaches, we hope to provide valuable insights and guidance for policymakers, stakeholders, and the general public.

Lessons Learnt:

1. Acknowledging the urgency: One of the most crucial lessons learnt is the need to acknowledge and prioritise the urgency of addressing climate change. Climate change is not a distant threat but a present reality. The frequency and intensity of extreme weather events, rising sea levels, and

changing precipitation patterns are clear indicators of the impacts of climate change. It is imperative that policymakers and society as a whole understand the magnitude of the problem and take immediate action to mitigate and adapt to its impacts. Delaying action only exacerbates the challenges and reduces the scope for effective solutions.

2. Collaborative governance: Effective responses to climate change require collaboration and cooperation among various stakeholders. Governments, local communities, non-governmental organisations, scientists, and businesses must work together to develop and implement climate change policies and initiatives. In regions like the Mediterranean, the Gulf, and the Indian Ocean, where multiple countries share common challenges, regional cooperation becomes essential to address transboundary impacts. Governments can facilitate collaboration by establishing regional platforms and forums, encouraging knowledge sharing, and jointly developing adaptation and mitigation strategies. Engaging with indigenous communities and traditional knowledge holders is also crucial for holistic and inclusive decision-making processes.

3. Integrated approaches: Climate change is a multi-dimensional issue that impacts various sectors, including agriculture, water resources, coastal zones, and infrastructure. The lessons learnt emphasise the importance of adopting integrated approaches that consider the interconnectedness of these sectors. Implementing policies and initiatives that cut across sectors ensures a more comprehensive response and increases the resilience of vulnerable regions. For instance, integrating water resource management strategies with agricultural practises and coastal zone planning can help optimise resource use and reduce vulnerability to climate change impacts. Integrated approaches should also consider gender mainstreaming to ensure equitable and inclusive outcomes.

4. Building adaptive capacity: Enhancing the adaptive capacity of communities and ecosystems is crucial for effective climate change responses. This
means investing in infrastructure, education, research, and technology that
enable societies to adapt to changing conditions. Empowering communities to develop local adaptation strategies and providing them with access
to relevant information and resources are significant factors in building
resilience. Support can come in the form of grants, capacity-building programmes, and technical assistance to vulnerable communities. Additionally, establishing early warning systems, contingency plans, and climate risk
insurance mechanisms can help communities better prepare for and respond to climate-related disasters. Resilience-building efforts should prioritise marginalised and vulnerable populations to ensure no one is left
behind.

Best Practises:

1. Climate-smart agriculture: Promoting climate-smart agricultural practises is essential for sustainable food production and rural livelihoods.
Techniques such as agroforestry, crop rotation, precision farming, and
agroecology can reduce greenhouse gas emissions, enhance soil fertility,
and improve water management. These practises not only contribute to
mitigating climate change but also build resilience by ensuring food security and enhancing the livelihoods of farmers. Supporting farmers in
adopting climate-smart agriculture through training, financial incentives,
access to markets, and promoting local and indigenous agrobiodiversity is
crucial. Integrated pest management and the use of organic fertilisers can
also reduce the environmental impact of agricultural practises.

2. Renewable energy transition: Transitioning to renewable energy sources
is a crucial best practise in mitigating climate change. Investing in solar,
wind, geothermal, and hydropower technologies reduces reliance on fossil

fuels and decreases carbon emissions. Governments should establish supportive policies, incentives, and regulations to facilitate the deployment of renewable energy systems. Collaborative initiatives between governments, private sector entities, and international organisations can help leverage expertise and funding for the development of renewable energy projects. Promoting distributed renewable energy systems, promoting energy efficiency, and fostering research and development in renewable energy technologies are key elements in achieving a clean energy transition.

3. Ecosystem-based adaptation: Preserving and restoring ecosystems not only secures biodiversity but also provides essential services in climate change adaptation. Coastal wetlands, mangroves, seagrass meadows, and coral reefs act as natural buffers against storm surges, sea-level rise, and erosion. Implementing ecosystem-based adaptation strategies can enhance resilience, promote sustainable livelihoods, and protect vulnerable communities. Integrated coastal zone management, including the protection of ecosystems and sustainable fisheries practises, can be achieved through partnerships between governments, local communities, and conservation organisations. These partnerships should incorporate traditional ecological knowledge and local practises to ensure the successful implementation of ecosystem-based adaptation measures. Supporting the establishment of marine protected areas and promoting sustainable tourism practises can safeguard marine ecosystems.

4. Public awareness and education: Promoting public awareness and understanding of climate change is vital to mobilise action and drive behaviour change. Educational campaigns, public outreach programmes, and school curricula should incorporate climate change as a core topic. Raising awareness about the importance of individual actions, such as reducing carbon footprints, sustainable consumption, waste reduction, and supporting local and ethical businesses, can foster a culture of sustainability.

Governments, media organisations, and civil society groups can collaborate to develop targeted communication strategies that utilise various media platforms to engage the public and promote sustainable behaviours. Engaging with the arts, storytelling, and indigenous knowledge systems can also be effective in conveying the urgency and interconnectedness of climate change issues.

Conclusion:

The lessons learnt and best practises identified in this chapter provide a roadmap for effective climate change responses in small islands and peninsulas. Climate change requires collective action, ongoing commitment, and transformative changes across all levels of society. By acknowledging the urgency, fostering collaborative governance, adopting integrated approaches, building adaptive capacity, embracing climate-smart agriculture, transitioning to renewable energy, implementing ecosystem-based adaptation, and promoting public awareness and education, we can forge a path towards a more sustainable and climate-resilient world. Let us learn from the past, embrace the best practises, and collectively work towards a future where the impacts of climate change are minimised, and the well-being of both people and the planet is prioritised.

Recommendations for Policy Frameworks

In light of the urgent and pressing challenges posed by climate change, it is imperative that robust and effective policy frameworks are established to mitigate its impacts and ensure the resilience and sustainability of our societies. This chapter presents a set of key recommendations for policymakers to consider when formulating policy frameworks to address climate change.

1. Integration of Climate Change in National Policies: Governments should aim to incorporate climate change considerations across all sectors and levels of policy-making. Climate change should be seen as a cross-cutting issue that requires a comprehensive and coordinated approach, involving various government departments and stakeholders. Integration can be achieved through the development of dedicated climate change strategies and action plans that align with national development goals.

- Integration of climate change considerations should involve assessing the vulnerability of key sectors, such as agriculture, energy, and transportation, to climate impacts. This will help identify priority areas for policy intervention and enable effective adaptation and mitigation strategies.

- Policymakers should also consider the social and economic dimensions of climate change, such as its impacts on livelihoods, poverty, and inequality, when integrating climate change into national policies. This will ensure a more holistic approach that addresses the needs and concerns of vulnerable populations.

- It is important for governments to engage with non-state actors, including civil society organisations, academia, and the private sector, in the integration process. Collaborative partnerships and multi-stakeholder dialogues can enhance the effectiveness and legitimacy of climate policies.

2. Strengthening Climate Governance Structures: Effective climate governance structures are crucial for the successful implementation of climate policies. Governments should establish clear lines of responsibility and accountability, assigning specific roles to relevant institutions and stakeholders. This includes the establishment of climate change departments or agencies, and the integration of climate experts in decision-making processes.

- Policymakers should ensure that climate change departments or agencies have adequate resources and authority to implement and enforce climate policies. This will help build institutional capacity and expertise, facilitating effective policy implementation.

- Mechanisms for monitoring, reporting, and evaluation should be put in place to ensure transparency and effectiveness in policy implementation.

Regular reporting on progress, including the achievement of targets and milestones, will enable policymakers to assess the effectiveness of their policies and make necessary adjustments.

- Policymakers should also consider establishing independent bodies or committees to oversee climate governance, ensuring cheques and balances and reducing the influence of vested interests. These bodies can provide unbiased assessments and recommendations on policy effectiveness, fostering greater accountability.

3. Investment in Renewable Energy and Sustainable Infrastructure: Transitioning to a low-carbon economy is essential for mitigating the effects of climate change and reducing greenhouse gas emissions. Policymakers should promote and incentivise the development and deployment of renewable energy sources, such as solar, wind, and hydropower.

- To accelerate the transition to clean energy, policymakers should establish clear targets and timelines for the deployment of renewable energy technologies. These targets can be supported by policy mechanisms such as feed-in tariffs, tax incentives, and renewable portfolio standards.

- Policymakers should prioritise research and development efforts in renewable energy technologies, including energy storage systems and grid integration solutions. This will help overcome barriers to renewable energy adoption and support the development of innovative solutions.

- In addition to renewable energy, policymakers should promote sustainable infrastructure development. This includes energy-efficient buildings, smart grids, and public transportation systems. The integration of climate considerations into infrastructure planning will ensure long-term resilience and sustainability.

4. Climate Change Adaptation and Resilience Building: Recognising the inevitability of climate change impacts, policymakers should prioritise and invest in climate change adaptation measures. This includes assessing vulnerability and risks, and developing adaptation plans and strategies that are context-specific.

- Policymakers should facilitate the mainstreaming of climate resilience considerations into all sectors and levels of planning. This can be achieved through the development of climate risk assessments, early warning systems, and measures that enhance adaptive capacity.

- It is crucial for policymakers to support the implementation of nature-based solutions for climate adaptation. This includes the conservation and restoration of ecosystems, such as forests, wetlands, and coastal habitats, which can provide multiple benefits, including flood protection, carbon sequestration, and biodiversity conservation.

- Policymakers should prioritise the protection of vulnerable populations, including marginalised communities and regions, to ensure that they are not disproportionately affected by climate change impacts. This can be achieved through the development of social protection programmes, access to finance for adaptation, and the provision of climate-resilient infrastructure in vulnerable areas.

5. Enhancing Climate Education and Awareness: To ensure widespread support and action on climate change, policymakers should prioritise climate education and awareness programmes. This includes integrating climate change topics within formal education curricula at all levels, as well as public awareness campaigns to foster behaviour change.

- Climate education should focus not only on raising awareness but also on building the necessary skills and knowledge for climate action. This includes promoting critical thinking, problem-solving, and decision-making skills that enable individuals to contribute to climate solutions in their personal and professional lives.

- Policymakers should support capacity-building initiatives that enhance the skills and knowledge of professionals in relevant sectors. This includes providing training programmes, workshops, and knowledge-sharing platforms that enable professionals to integrate climate considerations into their work.

- Collaboration with educational institutions, research centres, and non-governmental organisations can enhance the effectiveness of climate education and awareness programmes. Partnerships can facilitate the exchange of expertise, resources, and best practises, thereby supporting a more comprehensive and impactful approach.

6. International Cooperation and Collaboration: Climate change is a global challenge that requires international cooperation and collaboration. Policymakers should actively engage in global climate negotiations, and support initiatives such as the Paris Agreement and the United Nations Framework Convention on Climate Change.

- Policymakers should work towards the implementation of global climate goals and commitments, including greenhouse gas emissions reduction targets, adaptation plans, and financial support mechanisms for developing countries. Collaboration with other countries, regional organisations, and international institutions can enhance the effectiveness of these efforts.

- Policymakers should support technology transfer and capacity-building initiatives in developing countries to enable them to adopt climate-friendly technologies and practises. This can be achieved through financial and technical assistance, knowledge sharing, and the facilitation of technology transfer through partnerships and cooperation agreements.

- Policymakers should actively participate in global climate finance mechanisms, such as the Green Climate Fund, to support the implementation of climate actions in developing countries. Mobilising financial resources, both domestic and international, is crucial for addressing the financial barriers to climate action and supporting the most vulnerable communities to adapt and mitigate climate change.

In conclusion, addressing the impacts of climate change requires strong and effective policy frameworks. The recommendations outlined in this chapter highlight key areas for policymakers to consider when developing climate change policy frameworks. By implementing these recommendations, governments can play a crucial role in mitigating climate change impacts, promoting sustainable development, and safeguarding the future for generations to come.

Opportunities for Regional and International Cooperation

In the face of an increasingly challenging climate change scenario, it is evident that the global community needs to join forces in order to effectively address and mitigate its impacts. Regional and international cooperation is crucial in facilitating the necessary actions and strategies to combat climate change. This chapter focuses on exploring the opportunities for collaboration on a regional and international level, highlighting the potential benefits, challenges, and necessary steps towards achieving effective cooperation.

1. Benefits of Regional and International Cooperation:

Regional and international cooperation offer numerous benefits in tackling climate change. Firstly, it allows for the sharing of knowledge, resources, and best practises among nations, leading to increased efficiency and effectiveness in addressing climate change challenges. Knowledge sharing can take various forms such as research collaboration, technological exchange, capacity building programmes, and policy sharing. Developed nations can provide expertise, resources, and funding to developing nations, enabling them to implement sustainable solutions and adapt to the changing climate. This exchange of knowledge and resources helps bridge the technology gap and enables countries to leapfrog to cleaner and more efficient technologies.

Cooperation also encourages joint research and scientific collaborations, promoting innovation and the development of sustainable solutions. By pooling resources and knowledge, nations can undertake joint research projects that facilitate breakthroughs in climate science, technology, and adaptation strategies. This collaboration not only increases scientific understanding but also fosters a culture of innovation and sharing, where new ideas can be co-developed, tested, and scaled up.

Furthermore, by working collaboratively, nations can harmonise policies, regulations, and standards, facilitating a more consistent and unified approach towards climate change mitigation and adaptation. This alignment ensures a level playing field, avoids trade imbalances, and fosters the efficient use of resources. Regional and international frameworks, such as emission trading systems, can promote the adoption of common standards that incentivise emission reductions and facilitate the transfer of clean technologies. By coordinating efforts, countries can avoid duplication of efforts and achieve economies of scale, ultimately leading to greater efficiency and cost-effectiveness.

2. Challenges in Achieving Regional and International Cooperation:
While the benefits of cooperation are evident, there are challenges that need to be addressed. Firstly, the diverse interests and priorities of nations

often hinder consensus and cooperation. Each country faces distinct socio-economic, political, and environmental circumstances, which influence their perspective on climate change and their preferred mitigation and adaptation measures. Overcoming these different priorities requires open and inclusive dialogue, negotiation, and finding common ground based on shared goals and principles. It is important to recognise the unique challenges faced by vulnerable regions and ensure their voices are heard in decision-making processes.

Additionally, issues related to sovereignty, governance frameworks, and conflicts of interest can impede progress in joint efforts. Countries must address concerns related to sovereignty and fair burden-sharing to foster trust and build cooperative frameworks that respect the rights and responsibilities of each participating nation. International agreements and mechanisms should be designed to accommodate the diverse needs and circumstances of different countries, taking into consideration their historical contributions to greenhouse gas emissions and their capacity to address climate change.

Furthermore, financial constraints, technological gaps, and limited capacity in some regions may pose obstacles to effective collaboration. Developed nations must extend financial and technical assistance to support vulnerable regions in their climate change efforts, ensuring equitable participation and reducing disparities. Support can come in the form of grants, concessional loans, technology transfer, and capacity building programmes. Mechanisms like the Green Climate Fund can be strengthened and expanded to ensure a steady flow of financial assistance to countries that need it the most. Technology transfer, in particular, plays a crucial role in enabling developing nations to access and utilise sustainable solutions that aid in their adaptation and mitigation efforts. International initiatives should promote the transfer of environmentally sound technologies on fair and favourable terms.

3. Steps Towards Achieving Effective Cooperation:

To foster regional and international cooperation, it is essential to take concrete steps. Firstly, establishing effective communication channels, platforms, and forums is crucial for facilitating dialogue and exchange of ideas among nations. These platforms can include regional conferences, workshops, and joint research initiatives. Regular dialogues allow countries to share experiences, identify gaps, and align their actions for better coordination. Efforts should be made to include all relevant stakeholders, including governments, civil society organisations, academia, and the private sector. This inclusive approach ensures that diverse perspectives and expertise are considered in decision-making processes.

Secondly, creating incentive mechanisms such as financial assistance, capacity building programmes, and technology transfer can encourage cooperation and support vulnerable regions in their climate change efforts. Developed nations should provide adequate financial resources to developing countries to assist them in adopting greener technologies and implementing climate resilient measures. Climate finance should be channelled towards projects that have a transformational impact and directly contribute to sustainable development. Technology transfer, as previously mentioned, can bridge the gap between developed and developing nations, enabling the latter to access and deploy sustainable solutions that aid in their adaptation and mitigation efforts. International platforms and partnerships should be strengthened to facilitate the transfer of technologies, including through the establishment of technology banks and innovation centres.

Thirdly, developing a framework for monitoring and evaluating cooperative actions can ensure accountability and progress tracking. Transparency and accountability are essential to build trust and ensure the effective implementation of cooperative initiatives. Regular monitoring and evaluation mechanisms, supported by accurate data and information sharing, enhance the understanding of progress achieved, identify gaps, and enable necessary course corrections. It is crucial to establish internationally agreed-upon metrics, indicators, and reporting mechanisms that capture both mitigation and adaptation efforts. This data-driven approach facilitates the identification of best practises, the assessment of impacts, and the sharing of lessons learnt.

Lastly, strong leadership and political will are paramount in driving regional and international cooperation efforts forward. Engaging leaders to prioritise and promote climate action at all levels of governance is crucial. Leaders can inspire commitment, facilitate negotiations, and mobilise resources to push for effective cooperation. National governments should integrate climate change considerations into their policies, strategies, and development plans. They should also engage in robust dialogue within regional and international platforms, advocating for collective action and championing the needs of vulnerable regions. Leadership should not be limited to governments alone; the private sector, academia, and civil society organisations also have a crucial role to play in driving sustainable solutions and promoting cooperation.

4. Existing Models of Cooperation:
There are already successful models of regional and international cooperation that can serve as inspiration and guidance. For instance, the European Union (EU) has made significant strides in collective climate action through the establishment of shared policies and frameworks. The EU's Renewable Energy Directive, the Emission Trading System, and the Energy Efficiency Directive serve as examples of regional collaboration that have enabled the EU to reduce its greenhouse gas emissions and promote

renewable energy investments. In addition to policy harmonisation, the EU also facilitates capacity building programmes and knowledge sharing among its member states.

Similarly, initiatives such as the UN Framework Convention on Climate Change (UNFCCC) and the Paris Agreement demonstrate the potential for global collaboration. The UNFCCC brings together countries to discuss climate change issues, while the Paris Agreement sets out long-term goals and a framework for global action. Through the Paris Agreement, countries have committed to limiting global warming to well below 2 degrees Celsius and pursuing efforts to limit the temperature increase to 1.5 degrees Celsius above pre-industrial levels. Nationally Determined Contributions (NDCs) submitted under the Paris Agreement outline countries' individual climate targets and efforts. By learning from these models and adapting them to international contexts, countries can build on existing frameworks to enhance regional and global cooperation.

Examples of regional cooperation include the African Union's Great Green Wall initiative, which aims to combat desertification and land degradation in the Sahel region through a collaborative effort involving multiple countries. This initiative promotes the sharing of knowledge, best practises, and funding to restore degraded lands and promote sustainable agriculture. The Association of Southeast Asian Nations (ASEAN) has also prioritised regional cooperation on climate change through the ASEAN Agreement on Transboundary Haze Pollution, which addresses the issue of forest fires and transboundary haze in the region. This agreement promotes information sharing, technology transfer, and joint capacity building to mitigate the impacts of haze on public health and the environment.

On an international level, initiatives such as Mission Innovation and the Breakthrough Energy Coalition bring together governments, private sector entities, and philanthropic organisations to accelerate clean energy innovation and deployment. These initiatives facilitate research collaboration, technology transfer, and financial support for clean energy projects. The Global Green Growth Institute (GGGI) is another example of an international organisation that promotes sustainable and inclusive economic growth through green investments, capacity building, and policy support.

Conclusion:

Regional and international cooperation offer significant opportunities to address the challenges of climate change collectively. Through knowledge sharing, joint research, policy harmonisation, and financial support, countries can enhance their capacity to mitigate and adapt to the changing climate. While challenges persist, steps towards effective cooperation can be taken by establishing communication channels, creating incentive mechanisms, developing monitoring frameworks, and demonstrating strong leadership. By building on existing models of cooperation, such as the European Union and the Paris Agreement, countries can work together towards a sustainable and resilient future. Ultimately, regional and international collaboration is crucial in achieving global climate goals and ensuring a safer and more sustainable planet for present and future generations.

CONCLUSION

I n conclusion, the impacts of climate change on small islands and peninsulas in the Mediterranean, Gulf, and Indian Ocean regions cannot be ignored. This book has delved into an extensive analysis of the vulnerability of these regions to climate change, the socio-economic impacts they face, and the policy responses and regional cooperation needed to address these challenges.

Through the examination of historical climate data and projections, it is evident that these regions are already experiencing the adverse effects of climate change. Rising sea levels, increased frequency and intensity of extreme weather events, water scarcity, and ecosystem degradation are just some of the challenges that communities in these areas confront.

Small islands are particularly susceptible to the impacts of climate change due to their limited size, geographic isolation, and fragile ecosystems. The Mediterranean, Gulf, and Indian Ocean regions are home to numerous islands and peninsulas, each unique in its cultural heritage and ecological significance. Unfortunately, these regions also face significant climate-related risks, which highlight the urgent need for action.

Rising sea levels pose a threat to the very existence of some islands. As temperatures rise and ice sheets melt, seawater encroaches upon coastal areas, eroding land and endangering communities. The loss of land not only disrupts ecosystems but also undermines the socio-economic fabric of these regions, as communities that have relied on the land for their livelihoods are forced to adapt or relocate.

To mitigate the impacts of rising sea levels, coastal communities need comprehensive adaptation strategies that include measures such as coastal protection infrastructure, land-use planning, and community relocation plans. Implementing such strategies requires close collaboration between governments, scientists, and local communities. It is essential to involve stakeholders at all levels to ensure that decisions are socially, economically, and ecologically sustainable.

Extreme weather events, such as cyclones and hurricanes, have become more frequent and intense due to climate change. These events often lead to devastating impacts on small islands and peninsulas, including destruction of infrastructure, loss of lives and livelihoods, and disruptions in essential services such as water and electricity. Rebuilding communities and restoring infrastructure in the aftermath of these events pose significant challenges.

To enhance resilience to extreme weather events, a multi-pronged approach is necessary. This includes investing in early warning systems, developing robust emergency response plans, promoting resilient infrastructure design and construction, and integrating climate change considerations into urban planning. Additionally, improving disaster risk management capabilities and strengthening community preparedness and response mechanisms are crucial to reducing vulnerability and ensuring rapid recovery.

Water scarcity is a pressing issue for these regions, as freshwater resources become increasingly scarce due to rising temperatures and changing precipitation patterns. Small islands and peninsulas depend heavily on these resources for agriculture, tourism, and daily life. Dwindling water supplies not only jeopardise these vital sectors but also exacerbate social inequalities, as vulnerable communities struggle to access clean and safe water.

To address water scarcity, innovative solutions are needed. These can include rainwater harvesting, water desalination, wastewater treatment and reuse, and efficient irrigation techniques. Implementing such measures requires investment in infrastructure and technology, as well as capacity-building initiatives to ensure the sustainable management of water resources. Integrated water resource management approaches, taking into account the needs of various sectors and the ecological health of water systems, are critical for long-term water security.

Ecosystem degradation is a direct result of climate change and human activities. The unique biodiversity and delicate ecosystems of small islands and peninsulas are at risk of irreversible damage, impacting both the local environment and the livelihoods of communities dependant on natural resources. Coral reefs, mangroves, and coastal wetlands, which provide essential services such as storm protection and nurseries for fish, are particularly vulnerable to climate change impacts.

Conserving and restoring ecosystems is not only crucial for biodiversity but also for the well-being of communities. Implementing marine protected areas, supporting sustainable fisheries practises, and promoting nature-based solutions can help preserve and restore these valuable ecosystems. Additionally, raising awareness about the importance of biodiversity and the role of ecosystems in mitigating climate change can foster a sense of environmental stewardship among communities, leading to more sustainable practises.

Addressing these challenges requires comprehensive policy responses and regional cooperation. Governments, non-governmental organisations, and international bodies must work together to develop and implement appropriate adaptation and mitigation strategies. Policies should focus on sustainable and low-carbon development, integrating climate change considerations into various sectors, and engaging all stakeholders, including local communities and indigenous peoples.

Regional cooperation plays a crucial role in building resilience and addressing transboundary climate change impacts. By sharing knowledge, technology, and resources, neighbouring countries can collaborate on adaptation and mitigation measures, enhancing the effectiveness of their efforts. Platforms for dialogue and knowledge-sharing, such as regional conferences and working groups, should be established to facilitate this cooperation.

Furthermore, it is essential to empower communities to build their resilience and adapt to the changing climate. This can be achieved through capacity-building programmes, financial and technical support, and promoting community-based adaptation initiatives. Communities must be involved in decision-making processes, as their knowledge and experience are invaluable in developing context-specific solutions.

Education and awareness about climate change are critical components of any response strategy. By increasing climate change literacy, societies can better understand the risks they face and the actions they can take to minimise these risks. Education programmes should target not only children and youth but also policymakers, professionals, and the general public, fostering a culture of environmental responsibility and sustainable living.

Promoting research and innovation is fundamental for addressing the unique challenges faced by small islands and peninsulas in the Mediterranean, Gulf, and Indian Ocean regions. By investing in scientific research, policymakers can make evidence-based decisions and develop targeted solutions to mitigate and adapt to climate change impacts. It is crucial to facilitate knowledge exchange and collaborations among researchers, practitioners, and policymakers to foster innovation and actionable insights.

In conclusion, addressing climate change in small islands and peninsulas requires a multi-dimensional and holistic approach that takes into account the social, economic, and environmental aspects of these regions. By prioritising the well-being of communities, fostering regional cooperation, empowering local actors, and increasing climate change awareness, we can create a more resilient and sustainable future.

As we reflect on the urgency of the climate crisis, it is essential to recognise that our collective actions have far-reaching consequences. The impacts of climate change on small islands and peninsulas are not isolated events but interconnected challenges that require global attention. By embracing this challenge and taking bold action, we can pave the way for a more sustainable and equitable world for current and future generations. Together, let us forge a path towards a climate-resilient future.

Recommendations for Future Research

As the field of climate change research continues to evolve, it is imperative to identify areas that require further investigation to deepen our understanding of the complexities and nuances of this pressing global issue. This chapter focuses on providing extended recommendations for future research, aiming to fill knowledge gaps and guide policy and decision-making processes effectively.

1. Enhancing Long-term Climate Projections:

The development of more accurate long-term climate projections is critical for anticipating and addressing the challenges posed by climate change. Future research should prioritise improving climate models by incorporating a wide range of variables. This includes refining our understanding of oceanic and atmospheric interactions, feedback loops, and carbon cycle dynamics. By enhancing our knowledge of these factors, we can generate more precise projections of future climate scenarios and their potential impacts on various regions.

To achieve this, research efforts should focus on improving the representation of Earth system processes in climate models. This involves refining the parameterisations of cloud formation, precipitation, and atmospheric circulation patterns. Additionally, incorporating high-resolution data from satellite measurements, ground-based observations, and paleoclimate records can provide valuable insights into historical climatic variations, enabling better model calibration and validation.

Furthermore, in order to better inform local decision-making, it is crucial to refine regional climate models. These models should consider local-scale factors such as topography, land use, and spatial variability in weather patterns. By tailoring projections to specific regions, policymakers and stakeholders can make more informed choices regarding adaptation and mitigation strategies that address the unique challenges faced by different communities.

2. Strengthening Understanding of Local-scale Impacts and Adaptation:

While global-scale studies provide valuable insights, localised impacts and adaptation strategies require greater attention in future research. Understanding the specific vulnerabilities of communities, ecosystems, and infrastructure at the local level will allow for the development of effective adaptation and resilience measures tailored to the context. Future research should explore in-depth the socio-economic, cultural, and environmental factors that influence vulnerability to climate change.

To achieve this, interdisciplinary approaches should be employed, encompassing fields such as sociology, anthropology, economics, and geography. By incorporating social sciences and engaging with local communities, researchers can assess how climate change intersects with existing inequalities and power structures. This will help inform the design and implementation of inclusive and context-specific policies and strategies that address the root causes of vulnerability.

Furthermore, research should focus on understanding the potential for transformative adaptation, which involves systemic and fundamental changes in societies and ecosystems. This approach goes beyond mere adjustments and seeks to reconfigure existing systems to address the underlying causes of vulnerability and build long-term resilience.

3. Unravelling Social and Cultural Dimensions:

Climate change is not solely an environmental issue; it is deeply interconnected with society and culture. Future research should delve deeper into the social and cultural dimensions of climate change, recognising how climate impacts intersect with existing social and economic inequalities. Understanding how communities perceive and respond to climate change will aid in the design and implementation of appropriate policies and strategies.

Research in this area should investigate the social barriers and enablers for climate change action, including examining attitudes, values, and behaviours related to climate change mitigation and adaptation. By understanding the underlying factors that shape individuals' and communities' responses to climate change, researchers can develop targeted interventions and communication strategies to foster engagement and promote sustainable behaviours.

Furthermore, incorporating indigenous knowledge systems and traditional ecological practises is essential, as they offer invaluable insights into sustainable and culturally appropriate adaptation measures. Such research should be undertaken through respectful and collaborative partnerships with indigenous communities, embracing participatory methodologies and co-designing research agendas.

Additionally, exploring the impacts on marginalised and vulnerable groups, such as women, children, and the elderly, is crucial for promoting equitable and just climate action. Understanding the differential impacts of climate change on various social groups can help shape policies and interventions that address the intersecting dimensions of gender, age, socio-economic status, and other forms of identity.

4. Harnessing Technology and Innovation:

Technology and innovation can play a pivotal role in addressing climate change and fostering sustainable development. Future research should focus on identifying emerging technologies, such as renewable energy, energy storage, carbon capture and storage, and climate-resilient infrastructure. Evaluating the scalability, technical feasibility, and economic viability of these technologies will provide valuable insights for policymakers and investors.

Furthermore, exploring the potential of emerging digital technologies, such as artificial intelligence, big data analytics, and the internet of things, can enable more effective monitoring, early warning systems, and decision-making processes. These technologies offer opportunities to enhance climate modelling, real-time data collection, and remote sensing, supporting adaptive management approaches.

Research in this field should also investigate the social and environmental dimensions of technology deployment. Understanding the potential risks, unintended consequences, and ethical considerations associated with emerging technologies is crucial for responsible innovation. Additionally, exploring ways to bridge the digital divide and ensuring equitable access to technological solutions will be essential to avoid exacerbating existing inequalities.

Collaborative research efforts between academia, industry, and policymakers will be essential in developing and implementing innovative solutions that can drive the transition to a low-carbon and climate-resilient future.

5. Assessing Health Impacts and Risks:

Climate change has significant implications for human health, both directly and indirectly. Future research should focus on understanding and addressing the complex links between climate change and health outcomes. This includes investigating the spread of infectious diseases, shifts in disease vectors, mental health impacts, heat-related illnesses, food and waterborne diseases, and overall public health system resilience.

Research in this field should adopt a multidisciplinary approach, integrating expertise from the fields of epidemiology, public health, climate science, and social sciences. By combining various data sources and methodologies, researchers can provide a comprehensive assessment of the impacts of climate change on human health.

Moreover, research should explore the differential health impacts on vulnerable populations, such as those living in poverty, children, the elderly, and communities with limited access to healthcare. Understanding the social determinants of health and the potential for climate change to exacerbate existing inequalities is crucial for developing effective adaptation and mitigation strategies.

Additionally, research should examine the co-benefits of climate action on health, such as reduced air pollution and improved access to clean water and sanitation. By quantifying these co-benefits, decision-makers can make more informed choices that promote both climate resilience and public health.

6. Evaluating Economic and Financial Considerations:

The economic and financial dimensions of climate change need to be further explored to support informed decision-making processes. Future research should evaluate the costs and benefits of various mitigation and adaptation strategies across different sectors of the economy. This includes assessing the economic implications of transitioning to a low-carbon economy, estimating the financial risks associated with climate change impacts, and exploring ways to mobilise climate finance at the necessary scale.

To achieve this, research should prioritise the development of comprehensive integrated assessment models that encompass economic sectors, social factors, and environmental considerations. These models should consider both short-term and long-term economic impacts, incorporating scenarios with varying levels of climate mitigation and adaptation efforts.

Research should also investigate innovative financing mechanisms that can unlock resources for climate action, particularly in developing countries. This may involve exploring the potential of blended finance, green bonds, carbon pricing mechanisms, and public-private partnerships. Additionally, understanding market dynamics, regulatory frameworks, and risk assessment methodologies will help in designing effective financial instruments and mobilising private sector investments.

Furthermore, research should assess the potential for green job creation, economic the development of sustainable industries. By understanding the economic opportunities associated with climate action, policymakers can promote innovation, job creation, and inclusive economic growth.

7. Strengthening International Collaboration and Governance:

Addressing the global challenge of climate change requires strong international collaboration and effective governance mechanisms. Future research should focus on evaluating existing international agreements, such as the Paris Agreement, and identifying opportunities for strengthening global climate governance.

Research in this area should explore ways to enhance transparency, accountability, and compliance with climate commitments. This includes assessing the effectiveness of monitoring, reporting, and verification mechanisms, as well as exploring options for enhancing international cooperation, knowledge sharing, and capacity building.

Furthermore, research should investigate the potential for international collaboration on technology transfer, financing, and capacity building for developing countries. Understanding the barriers and opportunities for technology transfer and fostering collaboration between developed and developing countries will be essential for ensuring a just transition to a low-carbon economy.

In addition, research should explore the potential of regional and sub-national governance mechanisms in driving climate action. Understanding the role of cities, states, and provinces in implementing climate policies and initiatives can provide valuable insights for scaling-up local and regional efforts.

8. Exploring Nature-based Solutions:

Nature-based solutions offer a cost-effective and sustainable approach to addressing climate change. Future research should focus on exploring the potential of nature-based solutions, such as reforestation, ecosystem restoration, and sustainable land management, in mitigating greenhouse gas emissions and enhancing climate resilience.

Research in this area should assess the co-benefits of nature-based solutions for biodiversity conservation, water resource management, and sustainable livelihoods. Understanding the ecological and socio-economic implications of these interventions will help in designing and implementing effective strategies that maximise multiple benefits.

Moreover, research should investigate the potential of nature-based solutions in urban areas, such as green infrastructure and urban forestry, in enhancing climate resilience and improving quality of life. Understanding the effectiveness of these interventions in reducing urban heat island effects, improving air and water quality, and promoting human well-being is crucial for sustainable urban development.

Conclusion:

Addressing the complex challenges of climate change requires a multidisciplinary and holistic approach. The recommendations outlined in this chapter highlight key areas for future research, aiming to deepen our understanding of climate change impacts and inform effective adaptation and mitigation strategies.

By enhancing long-term climate projections, strengthening understanding of local-scale impacts and adaptation, unravelling social and cultural dimensions, harnessing technology and innovation, assessing health impacts and risks, evaluating economic and financial considerations, strengthening international collaboration and governance, and exploring nature-based solutions, we can make significant progress toward building a more sustainable and resilient future.

It is important to prioritise research that is inclusive, participatory, and context-specific, ensuring the voices of marginalised communities and indigenous peoples are heard and their knowledge is valued. By engaging in collaborative research efforts and sharing knowledge across disciplines and regions, we can collectively address the challenges posed by climate change and work towards a more sustainable and equitable world.

Call to Action for Policymakers and the General Public

In the face of the escalating climate crisis, it is imperative for policymakers and the general public to take immediate and decisive action. While the gravity of the situation may feel overwhelming, it is essential to remember that we have the power to shape our future. This chapter serves as a call to action, laying out the responsibilities and necessary steps that both policymakers and the general public must take to address climate change effectively.

1. Acknowledge the Urgency:

Policymakers and the general public need to recognise the urgent need for action. Climate change is not a distant threat but a present reality, impacting communities and ecosystems worldwide. Ignoring or downplaying its significance will only exacerbate its consequences. By acknowledging the urgency, we can begin to mobilise resources, implement policies, and engage in initiatives that address climate change head-on.

The scientific consensus is clear: human activities, particularly the burning of fossil fuels, are the primary drivers of global warming and climate change. These activities release greenhouse gases into the atmosphere, trapping heat and causing the Earth's temperatures to rise. The consequences of climate change are far-reaching, including rising sea levels, extreme weather events, loss of biodiversity, and disruptions to economies. Failure to act swiftly will lead to irreversible damage to our planet and future generations.

2. Implement Strong Policy Measures:

Policymakers hold a key role in driving meaningful change. They must prioritise the implementation of robust policy measures that promote sustainability, reduce greenhouse gas emissions, and foster resilience. This includes developing stringent regulations, incentivising green technologies, and investing in renewable energy sources.

To achieve a sustainable future, policymakers should prioritise the phase-out of fossil fuel subsidies and redirect those resources towards renewable energy research, development, and deployment. They can also introduce carbon pricing mechanisms, such as carbon taxes or emissions trading systems, to internalise the costs of greenhouse gas emissions and encourage sustainable practises.

Furthermore, policymakers should work towards creating a conducive environment for sustainable innovation and entrepreneurship. This includes providing funding support, tax incentives, and regulatory frameworks that promote the adoption and scaling-up of sustainable technologies.

Additionally, policymakers must ensure that climate change adaptation strategies are integrated into development plans and policies across sectors. This would involve assessing vulnerability and developing strategies to protect vulnerable populations, ecosystems, and infrastructure from the impacts of climate change.

Moreover, policymakers should address the social and economic dimensions of climate change to ensure a just and equitable transition. This includes investing in job creation and retraining programmes in renewable energy industries, supporting affected communities and workers in transitioning away from carbon-intensive sectors, and advocating for income redistribution to mitigate the impacts of climate change on marginalised and vulnerable populations.

3. Foster International Cooperation:
Climate change is a global challenge that requires international cooperation and collaboration. Policymakers should actively engage in multilateral efforts, such as international climate agreements, to collectively work towards reducing emissions and adapting to the impacts of climate change.

The Paris Agreement, adopted by 195 countries, represents a significant step towards global cooperation in combating climate change. Policymakers must adhere to their commitments under this agreement and strengthen their efforts to limit global warming below 1.5 degrees Celsius compared to pre-industrial levels. This will require revision and enhancement of the Nationally Determined Contributions (NDCs), which outline each country's efforts to reduce emissions. Policymakers should also contribute financially to support developing countries in their climate change mitigation and adaptation efforts.

Additionally, international collaboration should extend to technology transfer and capacity-building initiatives. Developed countries should assist developing countries in adopting and implementing sustainable technologies by providing financial and technical resources.

4. Raise Climate Change Awareness:

The general public plays a crucial role in addressing climate change. Increasing public awareness and understanding of the issue is essential in driving individual and collective action. Policymakers and stakeholders should actively invest in educational campaigns and initiatives that promote climate change literacy, highlighting the interconnectedness between human activities and the environment. This will encourage sustainable lifestyle choices and foster a sense of responsibility towards addressing climate change.

Education should be integrated into school curricula at all levels, ensuring that students are equipped with the knowledge and skills necessary to tackle climate change. Public awareness campaigns, through various media platforms, should be accessible, accurate, and engaging. These campaigns should emphasise the link between personal actions and their impact on the environment, making individuals realise that their choices matter.

Moreover, climate change communication should focus not only on the risks and challenges but also on the opportunities and co-benefits of addressing climate change. By highlighting the potential for job creation, economic growth, and improved public health, policymakers can inspire proactive actions among the general public.

5. Encourage Sustainable Practises:

Beyond awareness, the general public must be encouraged to adopt sustainable practises in their daily lives. Policymakers can support this by providing incentives and infrastructure that promote the use of public transportation, renewable energy, and waste reduction. Additionally, individuals and communities should be encouraged to engage in sustainable agriculture, conservation efforts, and responsible consumption practises.

Policymakers should invest in building sustainable and resilient cities, with efficient public transportation systems, green spaces, and infrastructure that recuces energy consumption. They should also incentivise the adoption of energy-saving measures, such as energy-efficient appliances and buildings, to reduce energy demand.

Individuals must be encouraged to make sustainable choices in their consumption patterns, favouring products with low carbon footprints and supporting companies that prioritise sustainability. By reducing meat consumption, making conscious choices about water usage, and minimising waste production, individuals can significantly contribute to mitigating climate change.

Furthermore, policymakers should promote sustainable agricultural practises that minimise greenhouse gas emissions, protect biodiversity, and ensure food security. This includes supporting regenerative and organic farming techniques, promoting agroforestry, and investing in research for climate-resilient crop varieties.

6. Invest in Research and Innovation:

To effectively address climate change, policymakers should prioritise investments in research and innovation. This includes funding interdisciplinary studies, technological advancements, and sustainable solutions. By supporting research institutions and fostering innovation, we can discover new methods to mitigate and adapt to the detrimental effects of climate change.

Policymakers should actively support scientific research on climate change, its impacts, and potential solutions. This includes funding research institutions, universities, and private initiatives that focus on developing and scaling up clean technologies, renewable energy sources, and carbon capture and storage methods. Increased investments in climate change research will not only lead to scientific advancements but also provide policymakers with evidence-based solutions for policy formulation.

Innovation should extend beyond technological advancements to include social innovation. Policymakers should support community-led initiatives, grassroots organisations, and indigenous knowledge systems that promote sustainable practises and enhance community resilience to climate change impacts.

Conclusion:

Addressing climate change requires the collective effort of policymakers and the general public. By acknowledging the urgency, implementing strong policy measures, fostering international cooperation, raising awareness, encouraging sustainable practises, and investing in research and innovation, we can work towards a sustainable and resilient future. Policymakers have a responsibility to enact meaningful change, while the general public must embrace their role as active citizens striving for a more sustainable world. Together, we can mitigate the impacts of climate change and secure a prosperous future for generations to come.

References For Further Reading

The following resources offer a variety of perspectives on climate change, from scientific analysis to socio-economic impacts and policy discussions. These works provide a comprehensive understanding of the multifaceted impacts of climate change in these specific regions and offer valuable insights into the challenges and opportunities for adaptation and mitigation. They are essential readings for anyone interested in understanding the regional nuances of climate change impacts and responses.

Specially For:

The Mediterranean Region:

"Climate Change 2022: Impacts, Adaptation and Vulnerability" by the IPCC.

This report includes comprehensive assessments of climate change impacts in the Mediterranean Basin. It addresses ongoing atmospheric and sea warming, projected changes in rainfall, and identifies the region as a 'climate change hotspot' with vulnerable natural systems and socioeconomic sectors.

The Arab Region:

"Adaptation to a Changing Climate in the Arab Countries" by Dorte Verner.

This book discusses the risks of climate change to poverty reduction and economic growth in Arab countries. It provides technical guidance on climate adaptation options for policymakers, covering economic impacts, water, health, tourism, biodiversity, disaster risk management, gender, and social relations. The report is a collaborative effort led by the World Bank and the League of Arab States, incorporating regional and international expertise.

The Indian Ocean Region:

"Heat and Freshwater Changes in the Indian Ocean Region" (Nature Reviews Earth & Environment).

This review article synthesises evidence from multiple data sources to examine the heat and freshwater changes in the Indian Ocean. It discusses the twentieth-century warming trends, the rapid rise in heat content since the 2000s, and the freshening over the eastern Indian Ocean and Maritime Continent. The article emphasises the need for sustained and enhanced observations, improved climate model simulations, and an integrated approach involving in situ observations, remote sensing, numerical modelling, and paleoproxy networks.

General

"All We Can Save" (Edited by Ayana Elizabeth Johnson and Katharine K. Wilkinson, 2020): A collection of essays, poetry, and art by women leading the climate movement, offering diverse ideas to advance the climate crisis conversation.

"How to Avoid a Climate Disaster" (Bill Gates, 2021): Gates shares insights from a decade of exploring the effects of climate change, focusing on necessary steps to stop environmental disaster and presenting a zero-emissions plan.

"Drawdown" (Paul Hawken, 2017): A comprehensive analysis of 100 climate change solutions, ranking them according to their benefits and presenting a path forward to invert the curve of carbon emissions.

"This Changes Everything" (Naomi Klein, 2015): Klein challenges the current economic system and its impact on the climate, advocating for reducing carbon emissions as an opportunity to rebuild local economies and reduce inequalities.

"Losing Earth" (Nathaniel Rich, 2019): A chronicle of the critical period between 1979 and 1989 in climate activism, exploring the birth of climate policy misinformation by the fossil fuels industry.

"Windfall" (Mckenzie Funk, 2015): Funk reports on how humanity might adapt to climate change, investigating those who profit from an ever-changing world and the implications for the planet.

"Don't Even Think About It" (George Marshall, 2015): Marshall explores why people deny climate change and how our evolutionary psychology influences our response to this global challenge.

Here are more categories of resources, along with specific sources within each category:

Internet Sources:
1. **NASA Climate Change**: NASA's Climate Change website offers valuable information, including satellite data, research articles, and visualizations related to climate change in the specified regions.
   - Website: [NASA Climate Change](https://climate.nasa.gov/)

2. **Pew Research Center - Climate Change and Global Warming**: Pew Research Center provides reports and surveys on public attitudes towards climate change in different regions, which can offer additional insights.
   - [Pew Research Center - Climate Change](https://www.pewresearch.org/topic/climate-environment/)

3. **National Geographic - Climate Change**: National Geographic provides articles, maps, and multimedia content covering the impact of climate change on the Mediterranean, Gulf, and Indian Ocean regions.
   - Website: [National Geographic - Climate Change](https://www.nationalgeographic.com/environment/climate-change/)

4. **Intergovernmental Panel on Climate Change (IPCC)**: The IPCC offers comprehensive reports and assessments on climate change, including regional impacts in the areas you're studying.

- Website: [IPCC](https://www.ipcc.ch/)

5. **World Bank - Climate Change Data Portal**: The World Bank's Climate Change Data Portal provides data and reports on climate change impacts and adaptation strategies in the specified regions.
  - Website: [World Bank Climate Change Data Portal](https://datacatalog.worldbank.org/dataset/climate-change-data)

Books:
1. **"Climate Change in the Mediterranean and the Middle East" by Antonio Marquina and Daniel Druckman**: This book provides a detailed analysis of climate change in the Mediterranean region and its implications.

2. **"Climate Change and Food Security in West Asia and North Africa" by Shabbir A. Shahid**: This book explores the impacts of climate change on food security in regions like the Gulf and the Mediterranean.

3. **"Climate Change and Coastal Ecosystems" edited by Richard J. Nicholls and Andrew C. Scott**: This book includes chapters on the impact of climate change on coastal areas, which are particularly relevant to the Mediterranean region.

Articles:
1. **"Climate Change in the Indian Ocean Region: An Analysis of Regional Climate Models" by Sultan Hameed et al.**: This research article discusses climate change projections and impacts in the Indian Ocean region.
  - [Link to Article](https://journals.ametsoc.org/view/journals/clim/30/5/jcli-d-16-0797.1.xml)

2. **"Climate Change in the Mediterranean Region: Current State and Perspectives" by Marco Mancini et al.**: This article provides insights into the current state of climate change in the Mediterranean and its potential future scenarios.

- [Link to Article](https://www.mdpi.com/2073-4433/10/8/439)

3. **"Climate Change Impacts on the Arabian Peninsula" by Abdulaziz M. Al-Abdulkader et al.**: This article focuses on the Gulf region and discusses the impacts of climate change, including extreme weather events and water scarcity.

- [Link to Article](https://www.mdpi.com/2225-1154/6/4/86)

www.ingramcontent.com/pod-product-compliance
Lightning Source LLC
Chambersburg PA
CBHW071052280326
41928CB00050B/2273